Hot Cross Buns

A Memoir

Anthony J Permal

Copyright © 2024 Anthony J Permal. All rights reserved.

The characters and events portrayed in this book are real, and some names have been changed to protect their privacy. Any similarity to other persons, living or dead, is coincidental and not intended by the author.

No part of this book may be reproduced, or stored in a retrieval system, or transmitted in any form or by any means, electronic, mechanical, photocopying, recording, or otherwise, without express written permission of the publisher.

Cover design by: Anthony J Permal / Dall-E / Canva

Contents

Dedication	IV
1. The Fastest Father	1
2. Of Incense and Milk Shops	12
3. Star Light, Star Bright: Merry Christmas, Alhamdulillah	35
4. Hot Cross Buns	46
5. Could You Please Turn to the Friendship Channel?	57
6. An Arrow to Your Heart	75
7. The Sacred and the Scared	82
8. School's Out	91
9. The Festival	115
Epilogue	125
Acknowledgements	129
About the author	131

For Dad and Mum

Chapter One

The Fastest Father

"The heart of a father is the masterpiece of nature." - Antoine Francis Prevost

Dad's running days really formed his body for life. Even after retirement, his lithe form, sinewy legs and lean muscled arms would gleam and bulge as if he had just returned from a long run. To my child's eyes, his physique always looked spectacular, never dulled by the familiarity of him being my father. The deep complexion shared by many Tamil Catholics in Karachi, intensified by the relentless sun of the coastal metropolis, often brought to mind a beloved athlete of mine, Carl Lewis. Lewis, an American with a similar dark skin tone, was a celebrated sporting figure known for representing his nation with pride.

It was the mid-20th century in Pakistan. John Permal was the pride and joy of the Christian community, for his success as runner. Born a Hindu in Karachi in May 1948, he was quickly baptised into Catholicism by his father, David, who had recently converted into the faith.

Hinduism and Catholicism were the two main religions of Pakistan's huge Tamil community, particularly in Karachi where most resided.

While the other great migrant Pakistani community, the Goans, had many icons like Charles Lobo, Hermond Raymond, and Dolores Almeida to be celebrated in the Christian community, Tamilians didn't have someone at this point in time. At least, not until John Permal graced athletics and shocked a continent with his speed as a runner.

The fastest human? A convert? In a Muslim country? This last bit would go on to have a major significance in his life when he retired. Until then, John Permal did what he always did: race to win. His love was the sound of his feet hitting the dirt. It made him feel alive, recognised and purposeful. It made him something off the field too: the eligible bachelor, the friend everyone wanted to pony up to, the icon that leaders wanted to rub shoulders with.

Years after this moment in time, I would be born. As I grew physically, so would my curiosity about his athletic career. One day, I'd ask Dad why his thighs weren't quite as thick as Carl's, which would prompt him to educate me on the difference between a sprinter who only runs the 100m dash and a long-distance runner which included those who run 200m races or 400m relays.

"What's a 400m relay?" I asked.

"It's when each team has not one but four people racing on the same track, starting at different lengths along the track. So, the first teammate starts, holding a baton. They race to the second teammate who's standing at the 100m mark, and hands them the baton. Teammate two races to teammate three, and so on until teammate four attempts to cross the finish line first. Four teammates, one race, 400-metres. A 100-metre sprint takes just one short burst of energy from you. But a 200-metre sprint is about endurance and having enough energy and muscle power to last that distance at speed, not unlike a cheetah," explained Dad.

"But you're only running 100m for a 400m relay. Isn't that the same?"

"Good point! It seems like it, but it isn't. Because you're not just focused on your feet this time. You're also focusing on not dropping the baton, on holding it tight, but also loosening your grip once you get close to your teammate on the track. Finally, you're focused on slowing down slightly so you don't run past them. It's not just speed for the 400m relay. It's endurance."

I marvelled at the explanations. Over the years, my eyes would still find their way to his thighs, which showed no evidence of the wear and tear that most retired athletes still carry beneath their taut skin.

The athlete, John Permal, was best remembered for his 100m sprints. But as his son, I know that his other love was the 400m relays—a category in which he won many medals.

Dad reached the peak of his athletic career between 1964 and 1974. He emerged victorious in various sprinting events, such as the Edinburgh Commonwealth Games, Thailand's Asian Games, the Dacca National Games (which was a part of Pakistan at that time), and Pakistan's own National Games. Additionally, he showcased his exceptional skills in numerous German track and field championships, consistently recording impressive times of 10.7 and 10.6 seconds in the 100-metres sprint. His remarkable performance at the Thailand Asian Games in Bangkok earned him recognition, admiration, and commendations from the Pakistani government and its people.

By the time I was born in 1979, Dad's athletic career had come to a close. However, he retained the habits of an athlete and the admiration of his community.

Even so, it was years after I graduated from childhood that I understood why dad walked for five or ten kilometres every day without breaking a sweat, and why his metabolism was like that of a cheetah. His body functioned on muscle memory—every cell fired up to burn food as fuel, pushing his energy, so he always felt like he was ready to go.

During my teenage years, I had a profound realization about my dad's willingness to assist others with their outdoor tasks. Despite his fondness for lounging on his floor cushion with a glass of Johnnie Walker while cheering for the Spurs, he would instantly jump into action whenever he learned that someone required assistance, walking the entire way. Dad didn't believe in using public transport unless it was at least five kilometres away.

"I have legs; I'm going to walk. It's just down the road!" He'd explain.

I could never tell if he was being helpful or if he just wanted to keep himself physically fit.

Dad loved telling stories from his life that made us laugh, wonder and even get bewildered. These included stories about his sporting career. One that always got me in splits was when he was in Germany in August 1971, representing Pakistan in a race in Berlin, accompanied by other Pakistani athletes and sports ministry folk.

One morning, they were waiting in the lobby of their hotel for the coach to take them for the race heats. One of the sports ministry officials ordered tea, and the hotel served it to him with a tea bag and hot water. The official steeped the tea with the tea bag, but then proceeded to remove the bag and start wringing it into the cup with his fingers like one wrings a washcloth to remove water. With others in the lobby looking at this, Dad and other Pakistani athletes got furiously embarrassed and asked him 'what the hell' he was doing.

He responded, "Oye yaar... maino apni cha taiz pasand ai... (Man, I like my tea strong)!"

The coach immediately reprimanded him. "Then order two or three more tea bags, you buffoon, instead of embarrassing the flag in front of everyone!"

My favourite story, however, was about one of Dad's victories. It's one he told me every year, without fail. There was an athletics championship in Peshawar, where the favourite was a local Pushtoon athlete who was also a good track and field star but was still growing.

Dad was the national champion already, so when he travelled to Peshawar from Karachi, everyone at home thought he would win. He said he did win the race and showed me the medal for it. But it was the toughest race of his life because. The Pushtoon favourite jumped the gun by a split second at the beginning, and surprisingly, no one acknowledged that it was a false start.

After Dad won and was walking to the locker room, he overheard the starting pistol man telling off the favourite. "I told you I'll give you a sign when I fire so you can start first, and you still lost? What was the point of helping you?"

It was a fixed match, which Dad still won because he was The Flash! It was his favourite story since it mattered more as he won fairly despite the odds stacked against him.

For me, the story highlighted another fact about Dad and all of us Christians: why we'd always be the 'others'. For Dad to not be treated like someone from the same country and rather 'the enemy' during that race is something I'd see echoed throughout his life, my life, and the lives of thousands of Christians in the 80s and 90s.

The overt religious extremist ideology that would be thrust upon us from the early 1970s would rear its ugly head, not just in daily life, but in sports as well. Dad often told us about how by the mid-seventies, Christian and Hindu athletes would often be sidelined in favour of local Muslim favourites, and in fact, he'd heard rumours of the authorities wanting to send an 'All Muslim Team' to the Olympics as well.

It's why I wasn't surprised when I grew up to see what happened to cricketer, Danish Kaneria, one of our best wicketkeepers who refused to convert. On the other hand, Yousuf Youhanna embraced a new name, Muhammad Yousuf, but unfortunately, he was eventually forgotten by those in power after he had served their purpose.

Dad would sometimes reminisce and tell us how he'd wished he'd immigrated to Canada when he'd had a chance in the late seventies, but he'd preferred to stay close to the country he loved. A country that never loved him back.

Growing up in the glow of your father's immense achievements makes all of this all the more relevant. It can be quite daunting, especially if you're fed all the information in one go.

Thankfully this didn't happen to me. My first exposure to Dad's incredible legacy was through Mum. She would tell us about Dad being the fastest runner in Pakistan, and then Asia. Her eyes would light up with excitement as she recounted how she would proudly stand in as the chief guest at sports events when he was away from the country.

As a child, it was hard to imagine that your father was ever younger than he presently was in your life. Dad? A boy? A young man? A teenager? Running? But he was always at his desk or on the floor watching The Spurs!

The full picture of Dad's life took form once we moved back to Karachi from Saudi Arabia where my father had taken up a job in 1977. It was after this move that we finally settled into our own home in Faria Apartments. Neighbours and guests would visit us and wax lyrical about how they used to watch Dad run in the stadium. It was my paternal grandmother, Magdalene Permal, who would tell us how it all started.

She told me and my sister, Sue, about how Dad walked almost three kilometres every morning, from Doli Khata to St Patrick's Boys' School—a Catholic school in Saddar. She narrated how this daily walk soon turned into running, and the running turned his legs into little rockets—at least, that's how she described them to five-year-old me. When the time came for him to take part in the weekly sports classes, his teachers saw him speed around the track like a bullet. The school took a special interest in Dad after that, nurturing his talent and giving him the attention, training and mentoring he needed to excel.

And excel he did.

His inter-school speed records brought him to the attention of the state, when Pakistan Railways heard of his speed times in the 100m and 200m dashes, as well as the 400m relays. They decided to scout and then drafted him to run for them at the national level. After this, he was selected to run for Pakistan as part of the international teams.

Over time, while Dad would tell us of all his achievements, I started hearing stories of his escapades from his best friends, Francis Rodrigues, Menin Rodrigues (who used to be Dad's student), Muhammad Alam, and my late beloved uncle and professor of Mathematics at DJ Sindh College in Karachi, Raju. They would fill in all the bits that were missing in Dad's and others' stories, especially the parts about how he got all the ladies!

In fact, it was Uncle Raju who told me that during his heyday as a sprinter, Dad would sometimes be a bouncer at KGA's parties. Young men would curry his favour to get into the party if they didn't have a lady on their arm, and young women would simply want to date him.

All of the above only foreshadowed a special day that would come years later during my teenage years. That day, I opened an old suitcase in the storage room of our home, curious to know what was inside. I discovered an old Dawn newspaper, its pages yellowed with age. It had the headline "John Permal, Fastest in Pakistan" emblazoned across the top.

I will probably never know the entire story of Dad's sporting career. Aside from personal stories, some photographs and countless certificates of achievement from around the world, there exists no reliable body of athletic work in Pakistan that chronicles the lives of our great sportsmen. Dad is only one of many hundreds of Pakistan's Olympians who simply don't exist beyond our stories and a few mementoes today.

Let's talk about hair.

Dad loved every hair on his head. He'd brush it to fluff it up, but never comb it. Dad's hair was beautiful, strikingly black, straight and silky, naturally sweeping backwards towards his nape. It enhanced his face, which was long, unlike mine which is more rounded. The long countenance was further highlighted by his chiselled nose, which was sharp and straight, and unlike mine. I wonder if this is why he hated facial hair. He never liked moustaches or beards, and all his life, he had one key habit: a clean, razor shave every single morning... rain or sunshine; work or weekend. His face was silky-smooth, just like his hair! Well, all except for his thick eyebrows, which I always wondered about.

When Dad grew older, he started using hair colouring, which I found funny because he looked wonderful on the rare occasions I saw his grey hair sprouting. But dark hair made him happy and confident. Whenever he came out of the bathroom with freshly washed, dyed hair, his mood was one of positivity and zeal. I found this fascinating about him. It's probably why he continued shaving until the very end.

His hair was a feature during his racing days, but second only to one other, more important thing—his sunglasses. Every photograph of Dad running showed him speeding across the finish line with his sunglasses firmly planted on his face, and his hair swept back in the wind. I asked him about this once and he simply replied, "I like sunglasses. I don't know why, but I can't run without them."

I know why, today. Symbols and traditions were important to Dad. The hair, sunglasses, sitting on the ground to eat or watch a match, collection of news story clippings... they were all habits that made him confident in himself—the routine which gave him self-esteem.

He wanted to be in control of his life and his results. Which is why the disease that took him away was so disheartening for him. Pancreatic cancer has no cure or treatment, except palliative care, and there was nothing he could prepare for, or change. No hair, no sunglasses, no newspapers; just his stories.

Dad recounted stories often, even though we had heard them a thousand times. Perhaps the most resounding of all his stories were about the legacy no one liked to talk about—Pakistan's failure as regards sports and sports heroes.

Dad would always talk about his final days as a runner, specifically referring to the gradual influence of Islamisation in the 1970s. He would mention how this shift affected various industries and fields, including athletics, as it seemed that there was a growing emphasis on promoting Muslim athletes over non-Muslims.

Since Christians were a dominant force in the track and field sports options, they were hit hard by this development. One of the stories he often spoke about with great sadness was the state of the official athletics stadium and grounds in Karachi. Throughout the 1980s and 1990s, it deteriorated into a neglected wasteland filled with potholes and overgrown with weeds, despite receiving funding from taxpayers through the Ministry of Sports.

Where the funds were going, he'd say, was something everyone knew but no one could do anything about. Dad asked a couple of times if the state would like his help in reviving the once-globally renowned athletics of Pakistan, but the state, as usual, declined and preferred obscurity to success.

He'd often scoff at the TV set whenever PTV broadcasted the Olympics, as he noticed that during the opening ceremony, there were often more overweight Pakistani sports officials marching than actual Pakistani athletes.

"They can't even walk without waddling, more nihari than nutrients!" is a comment I'd hear every four years. "Look at that one, he looks like he ate the rest of the team and decided to attend himself!" was another of his favourite statements.

Feet, hair, nose, thighs, skin... I knew every inch of my father's body. Every freckle and wrinkle; every tooth in his smile and dip in his muscles. His expressions in any situation are etched into my mind. That is why I can never forget the look on his face every time he saw the state of his beloved sport in the country, or when DHL Pakistan released a calendar in the nineties, celebrating Pakistan's athletics heroes of an era gone by.

John Permal—the fastest man in Pakistan and the pride of the nation, who won against all odds—was not among them.

Chapter Two

Of Incense and Milk Shops

> "Perhaps home is not a place, but simply an irrevocable condition" - James Baldwin

Incense!

I was in my 'toy room' playing with my GI Joes when the sweet aroma hit my nose. Sue and I called it the toy room, but it was just the second bedroom of our home in Saudi Arabia, which Mum and Dad converted into a play area and guest room because Uncle Jerry and Aunty Maggie stayed over some weekends.

Uncle Jerry was Dad's best friend, and Aunty Maggie was Sue's godmother. I didn't know what godmothers were supposed to do, but I knew she kept giving Sue gifts every other month. My godmother never gave me anything. I guessed she was not like God.

The aroma hit me first before Sue registered it. It was prayer. Mum's daily ritual was incense at 6pm. Dad reached home from work at exactly 5:10pm every day, and at 6, the incense that marked the beginning of family teatime wafted through our home.

Dad had moved to Saudi during the migration of young men in the late 70s to the newly oil-booming economy of the Kingdom. After his sporting days were done, employment in a decent job was the way of the world for sportsmen, and he chose the travel industry. My father worked for Kanoo Travels in Dhahran, creating a life full of travels and family time abroad for us, young ones.

Dad was a man of routine. At 6pm, sharp, Dad, Mum, Sue and I sat in front of the altar. Well, we called it an altar. It was Saudi Arabia; we had to make sure that like all other Catholics, our religious items could be easily dismantled and hidden away. At least, that's what Mum told me. So, Dad placed a bedsheet over a trunk in the corner of the bedroom and placed a painting of Jesus on it with a statue of Mother Mary in front of it.

Being 4 years old, I had learned the prayers by rote—the 'I Believe', 'Our Father', and the 'Hail Marys'. As always, Dad led the Litany. I always enjoyed Dad's litanies—his powerful, booming, yet restrained voice, articulating each word and phrase with the dignity it requested.

Looking up at him as he read, I felt like Jesus was personally listening to him, and if I tried and prayed hard enough, He would listen to me too. As for my prayers, there was really only one thing I wanted—to never return to Karachi. But I had been told that that was inevitable.

It was one of those things you couldn't reconcile as a child. There were things I loved about Karachi—the family, the presents that family would bring us, and the celebrations of Christmas, Easter and birthdays with large groups of my friends from the Parish. But what made me prefer Saudi were the things we enjoyed which weren't prominent in Karachi. These things included air-conditioning, cleanliness on the streets, amazing shopping malls, places we'd only seen in movies—McDonald's, Pizza Hut— and American and British TV channels like the BBC, which played songs I'd never heard before.

I enjoyed the community spirit of Karachi, but I longed to stay in the wonders of Saudi Arabia that I was exposed to. After all, Saudi Arabia was where I had my first real cheeseburger and deep-dish pizza, and also where I got exposed to The Bee Gees.

Our home in Al Khobar was perfect. It had three air conditioners, a toy room, and a separate room for Sue and me to sleep and play in. It was a walkable distance from the beach and every other thing we liked. The house had a wooden cabinet where Dad kept our Kellogg's and Trix cornflakes. The scent of fresh wood lingered in the cabinet, as if it had just been cut from the tree. I think that's why every time we were to fly to Saudi for school holidays, I would smell wood in the air, no matter where I was.

Downstairs, the grocery store was run by Raju who hailed from Kerala in India. I only recently learned that that was his name, as everyone called him 'naheen hai', which was Urdu for 'Don't have'. That was because every time we asked him for anything, he would bob his head the way South Indians do and say "Naheen hai!"

"Well, what do you have, Raju? You're running a damn grocery store, aren't you?" Mum asked him every day.

The best thing about the apartment, however, was the fact that it was across the road from the beach. We couldn't wait for Friday because it meant that by Thursday night, all of Mum and Dad's friends would come for a sleep-over and bring their kids too. The next day, being Friday, we'd all wake up early, walk to the beach and jump into the water, except when there were weird, long brown leafy things floating around. Dad called them seaweeds, but I think they were eels. Why would the sea have weeds? Isn't so much salt bad for leaves?

Yet, somehow, Dad often brought home tickets, and we kept flying back to Pakistan. One of these times, I knew we'd go back for good. The only thing I found similar in my two homes was the smell of smoke.

In Saudi, it was the incense. In Karachi, it was the sweet smell of smoke from freshly chopped tree trunks being turned into coal in Doli Khata. I wondered why they called it Doli Khata. I pictured a bank and a restaurant inside it because Mum told me Khata means eating, but it also means account. It didn't make any sense to me, but I can't recall why I didn't ask more.

Wood smoke... not incense anymore.

We returned to Karachi in 1984, and smoke drifted away from the burnt logs lying at the entrance to Bangali Parra, which was where Amma and Nyna, my mum's parents, lived.

Bangali Parra always felt more real to me than other places in Karachi. Somehow, no one pretended to be someone else here. The Parra was a huge, enclosed compound with one-room homes along the walls, and one storey above the ground for more homes.

Amma and Nyna had a home on the ground floor with a room on the inside, an open kitchen area on the outside, and a fence-like wall that my head barely reached. There was no door; everyone relied on a curtain for privacy. The bathrooms were outdoors too, with wooden or concrete walls around them and an open window on the roof for ventilation. Everything would disappear after we were done, and I never heard a flush. Amma is a magician, I always thought. Everything smelled like chilli powder, coriander and coconut... even the bathroom!

We were supposed to stay in Amma and Nyna's home for a bit, while Mum and Dad sorted out our new home. Father Robbie was helping them. Dad really liked Father Robbie. He was the priest who baptised me when I was born, and also joined Mum and Dad at the Metropole Hotel's Tavern Hall.

Mum said that Dad saved up for a few years for our home. "Now, we can buy our own place and you can get your own rooms!" I couldn't believe my ears. So far, the only time I had seen kids with their own rooms was on American TV shows. I was going to be like Punky Brewster!

I didn't want to leave my home in Saudi, but now that I was here, I didn't want to leave Bangali Parra, either. So far, I had learned that sixty families lived there. Their names were all different, though. Some sounded like our names—D'Souzas, Francis and Periera.

The people living next to us were called the Aziz family, which reminded me of the man on TV who gave away ceiling fans and water coolers to people who answered his questions. I wanted a water cooler too every time I saw that. But I never saw anyone win the fridge that was on stage with him.

Why was their family name so different? Mum said it was because they were Muslims. What are Muslims? Do they have different priests? Are they the ones who wake me up in the morning with their loudspeakers in the mosque? I didn't know, but I was sure that I'd find out.

The other families in the Parra had people called Ganga, Prakash and Naureen. Mum said they didn't go to Church; they worshipped at the Hanuman Mandir temple next door. It was the one where I saw the elephant and monkey statues, she reminded me. I found that interesting because in Church, we only had the donkey and cow statues during Christmas, but these people kept those statues up all year. Maybe they celebrated Christmas longer than we did. I wasn't sure, but it sounded amazing! I thought that I'd like living in Bangali Parra because of all the different food and candies I'd eat throughout the year.

Every month, it felt like someone else was celebrating Christmas; but in their own way. One of the families gave us meat once a year—a lot of meat—but they also brought kheer. I loved kheer. I never found any dessert in Saudi like it. That was probably why I loved the Parra.

Uncle Aziz was my favourite person in the Parra. He ran the laundry out of his home, and everyone went to him, including us, the kids. We only went to him because at 4pm, every day, he told us scary stories while ironing clothes with a coal iron! Sometimes, if we were lucky, he'd give us candy, but I thought he only did so because he wanted to eat some, too. I always noticed him tucking one piece of candy into his turban. He was probably hiding it from his wife.

In the middle of the Parra was my favourite thing in the whole wide world: a big black iron pipe sticking out of the ground, with a large handle on the side. Mum accompanied me, holding a large steel bucket. She allowed me to pump the handle repeatedly until clear water gushed out from the ground. She mentioned that there was a well underneath, but I was too focused on pumping the water to pay much attention. The more vigorously I pulled the handle, the more water flowed out. It was like magic.

Nyna surprised everyone in the Parra by bringing home a box one day, sparking excitement among the community members. Rumours spread that he had purchased a TV, but I found it hard to believe. In a house where no one owned a TV, Amma and Nyna were content with their beloved radio. Besides, with the record player, speakers, three cupboards, and a giant bed already taking up space, where would they even put a TV?

Nyna was correct, indeed. Upon opening the box, an incredible TV emerged, twice the size of my head. Placing it on the bookshelf, he switched it on, revealing that it was already set to PTV, displaying a TV show in Urdu. It was at that moment that I noticed something strange.

The label on the box indicated that the contents were black and white, however, the television program was displayed in colour. In fact, it showcased three vibrant colours: pink, blue, and grey. Nyna noticed my perplexity and asked me to come closer to the TV. He pointed to the corner of the screen and explained, "It's a sticker, Anton. The sticker is in three colours, and it's stuck onto the screen to make us think the images are in colour. Isn't that magical?"

I nodded, wide-eyed. I couldn't believe this was possible. A few days later, we returned home from the market at about 7pm and there was a crowd gathered outside. Mum got worried and rushed inside, only to see Nyna excitedly telling everyone to wait, as there wasn't enough room for so many. It turned out that Nyna's house had become the Parra's cinema. Everyone wanted to sit and watch the TV. So, Nyna had to figure out an arrangement. Every evening, a different set of five people would watch TV from 8pm until after the Khabarnama at 9pm. Children, however, as many as could fit inside, would be allowed to watch the cartoons that came on earlier.

My grandparents had their own 14-inch cinema at home! How was that for bragging rights when I got back to school?

Time flew by with all these shenanigans until one day in 1985, when Mum burst into the room with some papers and excitedly grabbed me and Sue. The papers of our new home had finally been signed. We were getting our own place!

In the heart of Cincinnatus Town, one kilometre away from Quaid-e-Azam memorial, Mum said there was a church called St Lawrence's. It was one of the oldest in Karachi, and it was surrounded by Catholics.

Garden East, they called it, was lined with pretty street names like Pedro D'souza Road, Britto Road, Love Lane, Vine Street, Rose Lane, Supariwala Street (which I honestly thought was a street of paan shops) and Chestnut Street. Our home was on a street called Maneckji, two blocks away from the church and three blocks away from the Ismaili Jamaat Khana.

It was called Faria Apartments and was only for Catholics. It contained 30 apartments—three blocks each of ten apartments across five floors. Dad managed to get us the biggest apartment: three full bedrooms, a living room and a lounge. It was at the top of the building, on the fourth floor. We could see the Quaid-e-Azam memorial from one side of the apartment and Habib Bank Plaza from the other side.

Upon moving in, we brought along only three sets of furniture: a bed where Mum, Sue, and I sleep together, and a sofa set consisting of one three-seater and two one-seaters, and a cupboard. Despite having just these items in our possession, we found contentment and joy in our humble abode. The security guard informed us that we were among the first families to settle in the area, alongside Sri Lankan immigrants, an Italian Catholic missionary group known as the Focolare, and a handful of other Catholic families.

Opposite our building, on the same piece of land but separated by a towering wall that rivals Mum's height, stood Taj Court. This five-story building housed only 20 apartments and accommodated a diverse mix of families.

There was a mosque opposite our house known as Pakola Masjid. I had a soft spot for Pakola, but I found it amusing that a mosque was named after a cola. Perhaps it was due to the green lights adorning the minaret? When my mum inquired with our neighbours, the Roques, they explained that the mosque was named after the Pakola Company, whose owners resided nearby on the same street.

Under Taj Court, we realised there was a grocery shop called Saeed Bhai's. Mum took us down there to buy milk for the morning, and the owner, Saeed Bhai, was sitting behind the counter. He looked old, like Nyna, but he had a bushy, white beard. Sitting next to him was another man who introduced himself to me as Uncle Afaq; he helped his father to run the shop. I could smell rice, atta and cinnamon in the air inside the shop. I liked it here. They had an entire row of candy in jars at the front counter!

My favourite place on our street, however, was the video shop. It was in a villa right next to the mosque and was run by Yaseen Bhai and Feroz Bhai. Inside, they had so many video cassettes that reached the ceiling, from the floor. Although it was a tiny shop, there were always people in there. The shop owners charged ten rupees per day for any video a customer rented. Mum told them that we would come back once we had a TV and video player because we didn't have them at the time.

I liked Faria Apartments. Something told me we were going to be alright. That was because I had yet to find out the place was haunted.

The Exorcism

One evening, Mum decided to have dinner at our home in Faria to celebrate Sue's fifth birthday. Every family member that she invited attended.

I was amazed to see our extended family members at the gathering—our cousins, aunts, uncles, grandaunts, and granduncles. It was surprising how they all knew my name and everything about me, even though I had never met them before. Among them was Uncle Moses, who was married to Dad's sister, making him Dad's brother-in-law. He had lost all his teeth due to old age. I found it quite amusing whenever he chewed something, as his jaw would close all the way up to his nose!

The dinner went on a long time, and since there were so many of us, kids, Mum allowed us to play for as long as we wanted. We watched cartoons, played in all the rooms and terrorised all the guests.

In the evening, Mum called out to me to help her with something, and I ran over to the kitchen where she was preparing dinner for everyone. She wanted me to get something from the bedroom which had a door to our large balcony. I quickly ran over to the room and switched the light on, looking straight at the open balcony door.

In an instant, I caught sight of a misty, ashen figure floating near the entrance, only to swiftly glide away and disappear from view. It took a brief moment for my mind to process what I had just witnessed—I had encountered a ghost. However, this was unlike the ones depicted in cartoons. It wasn't a classic white sheet with holes for eyes, but rather, a smoky presence, resembling the silhouette of a person. It resembled a person in a dream, simultaneously present yet intangible, distinct yet lacking a defined form.

I quickly grabbed what Mum wanted and ran to her, telling her what I saw. She came with me to the balcony, but called Uncle Augustine and her brother, whom we all called 'Baba'. They checked the balcony but didn't see anything. Someone said it was possible that I saw a ghost because a few people in the building had mentioned that they had each seen something, over the past few years.

Soon, Mum started to believe the house was haunted. She wasn't sure if they were good or bad spirits, and so she wanted to make sure there were no more scares.

It was important for Mum to make sure we didn't have any more such incidents, not just because she didn't want Sue and me to be scared, but because she was visibly pregnant. I had noticed her tummy growing more and more since Spring. I didn't know at the time that she was pregnant, I just thought she'd eaten a lot over Christmas.

She visited Fr Robbie at Church to tell him about it and asked if he could help. He suggested an exorcism at the house and began to prepare for it. He told us all to pray the Rosary and the Chaplet of the Sacred Heart to prepare our souls. I had no idea what all of these meant, and I didn't like praying the Rosary, but Mum insisted.

The next day, Fr Robbie arrived at our house holding a Bible, a small prayer book, holy water and holy oil. He also carried a Cross in his hand, but it looked different from other Crosses I had seen priests carry.

This one was made of thick wood and was about the size of a bottle of Pakola. It had strange markings etched into it, and a coin on each side of it, in the middle where the two wooden pieces converged.

He told me that the coins were medals of St Benedict, the Catholic saint known to have created the exorcism rites of prayer.

He began by calling us all to the altar in our home where Mum and Dad hung a large image of Our Lady of Health, as well as a picture of the Sacred Heart of Jesus. We began with the Sign of the Cross, and he started praying a decade of the Rosary, asking Mary to protect us.

I started to get a bit scared.

He then told us all to walk with him into each room and to not stray anywhere else in the house. We had to stay close to him at all times. He began reciting the exorcism prayers from his little book, holding the Cross up high, facing the middle of the room we were in. He did this in every room, including the bathrooms, kitchen, storage room and both balconies.

Before leaving each room, he sprinkled holy water onto its walls and rubbed holy oil into the doorway of the room.

By the time we were done, we went back to the altar room, and he suggested that we pray the Rosary together. This took at least fifteen minutes; by now, I was really tired and sleepy.

When we finished, he said that if there was anything in the house, it was gone now.

Mum invited him to stay for dinner, to which he obliged. Before we retired to bed that night, Mum told me that she had called the Hindu priest from the temple in Soldier Bazar to help too, and he'd be arriving the next morning.

I didn't know what a Hindu priest would do, but I soon found out.

The next morning, our cleaner Premi showed up at our home with a man dressed in red clothes, large beads around his neck, and a long white beard. His skin was dark brown and very wrinkled, like our clothes before they were ironed.

He was carrying a bag around his shoulder like a sack, which seemed heavy with something.

In our house, he sat in the middle of the living room, on the ground, and started to empty the sack. He brought out a statue of Ganesh, the elephant god of the Hindus, as well as statues of Krishna and a female goddess whose name I can't remember. I recognised Krishna's statue because it was holding a flute which I remember seeing in the Indian movies Mum usually rented from the video shop.

He also removed a number of incense sticks that he called agarbattis. He asked Premi and Mum to light them up and put them at the windows of every room.

He then proceeded to place all the statues in a row at the centre where he sat. He began to recite a variety of words that Mum told me were called Sanskrit, the language of the Hindus. I had never seen anything like this before, so I sat there mesmerized.

After a while, he took a stick of broom out of the sack and blew on it. He got up and started going into each room, reciting the Sanskrit stuff and waving the broom in deliberate motions at the centre. He did this in every room and got louder and more animated as we neared the balcony.

I believe Mum had informed him that that was where I had encountered the spirit. He emphasised the exorcism process there and lingered for a while, before eventually concluding and advising us to vacate the premises for a few hours.

We opted to visit Aunt Jacqui's residence, which I was excited about because I could spend time playing with their adorable new babies, Tammy and Tracy.

After a couple of days, Mum reached out to a third individual for help. This time, it was a Muslim exorcist who arrived with a goat, which I found to be quite strange.

Why is a goat in my house?

He didn't go through the elaborate rituals like the others before him. Instead, he quickly recited something upon entering our home and began to walk to each room, like the other priests did. He, however, took the goat with him, occasionally having to pull it by the horns.

When he was done, he left and mentioned that the slaughter would take place once he went downstairs.

Slaughter? Why does the goat need to be slaughtered? My mother explained that the goat had absorbed the negative energies in our house, and by slaughtering it, the spirits would be released to their rightful place.

I found that revolting, especially because the poor animal was probably just playing with its friends when this random man decided to make it a vessel for the devil's spawn. What a strange day for it!

Yet here we were… three religious ceremonies in a week to rid my home of the spirit I saw.

I felt relieved that I wouldn't have to see one again. I never did, after that day. I did, however, feel it.

A few years later, when I was fourteen, I was asleep in my bed, in my own room, as Sue and I now had separate rooms.

It was around 11:30pm. Mum and Sue were asleep, too. Before I slept, I had finished reading King Solomon's Mines—one of my favourite books in the whole world. For some reason, I really liked the author's name—Haggard. It sounded like the name of a rugged explorer. Leaving the light on, I climbed into bed and snuggled into my pillow.

Suddenly the sheet I'd draped over myself began to move. It felt like something was holding onto one end of it and was waving it up and down, so that it kept slapping my feet.

I was petrified! At first, I thought it might be because of the ceiling fan that was on at full oscillation. Slowly peeking out from under the sheet, I discovered that the fan was off. I had never turned it on.

I remember ripping the sheet off my body and rushing out of the room, with my eyes tightly closed so that I wouldn't see anything even if it were there.

That night, I slept in my parents' room after telling them my room was too cold.

By the next day, I had gotten over the feeling of shock and realised the three exorcisms would have gotten rid of whoever or whatever it was that was haunting – or taunting – me, and hence this spirit, whatever it was, was most definitely a good spirit.

I slept in my own room the next night, and the night after... and all nights after that, but never experienced anything ever again.

I guess the spirit realised it was no longer going to get a reaction out of me and decided to leave. It would only be months later that Uncle Ronnie told us that the villa behind our home, which was the giant property with acres of palm trees and vegetation, had a cemetery in the corner for the family's dead.

That explained a lot or left a lot to be explained. I guess I'll never know.

Jericho

Sue and I were suddenly awoken one August afternoon by Amma. Mum wasn't at home, and Amma insisted we quickly wash up and get dressed, as she was going to take us to see Mum. We were both confused. Where had Mum gone? Was something wrong? Did something happen to her? Wait, did she get back to Saudi? Are WE going to Saudi?

That last thought is what got us all really excited. We dressed up and ran to the door, waiting for Amma, who had gone into the kitchen and was filling up a bag with fruit and other nibbles. That's why Sue asked 'where is our luggage? Why didn't Amma pack any clothes for Saudi?'

I realised that too and ran into the kitchen to ask Amma what was going on. She told me to be quiet and wait, we would leave as soon as she was done.

Five minutes later, we were all rushing down the stairs, at the bottom of which Baba Mama was waiting with another friend in a car. We bundled into it, and they started driving really fast. 5 minutes later we were alighting at Holy Family Hospital which was near Doli Khata, and I suddenly got scared. Why are we at a hospital?

Amma smiled and said it's time for a surprise, and Sue wondered if we were going to get their famous chicken sandwich, the only thing the hospital canteen really had that was good enough to eat.

Amma spoke to the reception at the hospital, who seemed to know her by name. 'Violet, she's in this room', gesturing to the first room around the corridor. We walked towards it, and that's when I saw Mum on the bed, talking to a nurse. Mum was in a hospital gown, and Sue called out at which Mum looked towards us and said to Amma 'please take them out from here, they'll get scared', and then she turned to the two of us to say 'don't worry beta, I'm just going for a quick operation, I'll be back soon, ok?'. She sounded really tired and weary, and I wasn't sure if it was because she had taken some medicine, or if she was exhausted from something, or both.

I don't remember much about anything else that happened after that, there were just so many people from Mum and Dad's families all around us. I saw some women praying the Rosary in a corner. One of Dad's friends was talking to one of our neighbours from Faria Apartments while having a smoke outside.

Time just slowed, and Sue fell asleep on one of the benches in the corridor.

A few hours later, Nyena and Baba Mama both burst into the room Mum had been sleeping in, saying 'bacha salamat agaya!', and Amma turned to Sue and me to say 'you have a brother! Bhai ayah ai bhai'.

We were both stunned, but before we could process the news we saw Mum being wheeled back into her room on the stretcher. We rushed to her side as the hospital staff settled her into the main bed of the room and tucked her in. She was still groggy from the anaesthesia, Amma told us. I didn't know what anaesthesia was, but I knew it made people sleepy if this is what it did to Mum. I asked her if she was ok, and she turned to me and said 'yes beta, everything is ok. You have a baby brother. I'm going to sleep now as I'm really tired'.

Sue and I both gave her a kiss on her cheek as Amma informed us it was time to go home as Mum needed to rest and get stronger. She had a Caesarean section, Nyena told us. What's a Caesarean section, Sue asked to which Amma replied that it was how both she and I were born, where the surgeon cuts a small hole in the tummy of Mum and pulls us out from there.

That explains the scar I saw many times on Mum's belly.

We were quite excited as we got home. We have a brother! Sue and I couldn't stop talking about it. We kept dreaming up things we were going to do with him. Sue kept saying she would dress him up in her clothes and put Mum's makeup on him so he could look beautiful. I wanted him to grow up fast so that I could show him my Lego sets and He-Man figures.

That's when it dawned on me: neither of us knew our brother's name.

"Amma!", I called out, "what's his name"?

"I don't know, beta, your Dad has to tell us. He will call us tomorrow and let us know."

Sue and I exchanged grins, because this meant we'd get to talk to Dad soon.

Sure enough, the next morning, we were both up and dressed ready to go back to the hospital. Amma had made us 'jam bread', but with the hard bread the roti wala brings at 7am. She made it exactly like Mum did: slicing the bread into thick slivers and roasting them on the tawa in butter. When they were mildly softer and buttery, she would slather a layer of Mitchell's Golden Apple Jam – my favourite – and give it to me with chai.

Off we went to the hospital once Baba Mama arrived, and sure enough there was a crowd in Mum's room and outside in the corridor. If ever there was a gathering of Tamil culture in Karachi, it was there as my Mum showed off the third Permal child. 9 paternal and maternal uncles and granduncles, aunts and grand aunts, their wives, children and cousins on all sides. Neighbours from Faria Apartments, St. Lawrence's parish, a lot of the people from Bangali Parra in Doli Khata, and the two of us standing there in front of them as they ran over to congratulate us both.

"Mum, what's his name, tell us his name", I insisted. She smiled and looked down at us from the bed. She had been sitting upright, drinking something one of our aunts was holding up for her. She said Dad had called that morning from Saudi to talk about the name.

I was disappointed, I missed Dad's call. But Mum saw the look on my face and told me he had called on the hospital number, as the room didn't have a phone and he only had limited to time to talk.

"Dad said he wanted to give him a strong Christian name, and something from the Bible. We spoke for a bit and he told me your brother's name".

Sue and I were both listening, and we realised the whole room had gone quiet. Everyone else was listening to her too. Apparently, it seems she didn't tell anyone else what name they had decided.

"Adrian Joshua Permal. That's your brother's name. Adrian is a nice Christian name that not everyone has right now, and Joshua is the name of the Prophet who tore down the walls of Jericho with his voice. We really thought that name would be something your brother can get blessed by", and I heard a lot of people murmur 'wah, nice' and 'Adrian, good name'.

Adrian. I liked it. Joshua made it sound like he would have a white beard. But I didn't think too much about it at the time.

Adrian Joshua Permal.

And then I saw him. Someone had carried him from the baby ward into the room and the first thing I realised was that he was fairer than everyone else in the room except Mum. Dad had always had dark skin, which is what I received too. Sue got a mix of Mum and Dad's complexion, but Adrian it seems got everything from Mum. Even the hair. Sue and I had curly hair since birth, but Adrian's hair is smooth and silky and straight, something Mum was known for in the entire family.

We spent the next few hours in the hospital with Mum and Adrian, and eventually went home.

That night Sue and wondered where Adrian would sleep.

Adrian had been born on August 20 in 1987. Just a few days later was when I would be receiving my First Holy Communion at St. Lawrence's Parish. Dad and Mum decided to have Adrian's baptism on the same day and got permission from Fr. Evarist, because they knew the church would be too busy that morning.

Fr. Evarist would later become the Bishop and then Archbishop of Karachi, but back then he was our mild mannered, very intellectual parish priest. All the kids loved him because he always had something fun to teach us about Jesus.

The day of the First Holy Communion arrived, and Mum dressed me up in fine white clothes. A pair of white trousers, while shirt and a light blue ribbon tied around my bicep, as tradition would have it. Adrian had been put in a small white baby gown with lace flowing onto the floor when someone held him.

At 9am, all of us Communicants who were receiving the Sacrament for the first time were told to sit in the first few rows of pews in Church, and to pray. Evelyn, Brendon Lobo, Rodney D'souza and many other friends who were receiving with me just sat there and pretended to pray, giggling because someone kept pinching someone else's butt and they kept yelling at them to stop. Church can be funny sometimes.

At 9:15, Aunty Irene called out to me and told me to come to the Baptistry. I ran as I knew it was time to name Adrian in the Church!

We had the ceremony and as I turned back to go to the pews, I realised no one was there in Church any more. I had no idea where everyone had gone. I figured I might as well go and sit just in case they were all breaking some rules and had gone awry, and I'd be the good boy.

Suddenly, Aunty Irene came running up to me and said 'Go outside! Why are you sitting here? They are all waiting."

I quickly ran out of Church to see all the Communicants had formed two rows. Boys on one side, girls next to them in the other. Everyone had their hands clasped in prayer in front of them, as we'd been taught to do during classes for the Sacrament, and I ran to find my position.

The procession started at 9:30, and in the coming hour I finally welcomed Jesus, Body and Blood, into my life.

Although, the wine we drank didn't taste like blood. Thank goodness for that. It smelled funny too, not like the wine Dad used to drink when he came to Karachi. It was also very sweet. Dad's wine was never sweet, which is why I never liked it.

Unfortunately, we would never drink that wine again for a long time. I didn't understand why. We had received our First Holy Communion and drunk the wine, so why don't we drink it all the time? Mum keeps taking us for Mass every Friday, but we only have the wafer.

Was Fr. Evarist keeping the wine for himself?

Chapter Three

Star Light, Star Bright: Merry Christmas, Alhamdulillah

"When they saw the star, they rejoiced with great joy."
- Matthew 2:10

From 1985 to 1995, my best friends Jonathan, Murad (Bubloo) and I shared 'custody' of Faria Apartments and Taj Court. We were the young and the brave, staking a claim as children over our territory. These two apartment blocks, each four stories high, were some of the tallest buildings in Garden East in 1985. There was a law that didn't allow anything taller, so Jinnah's Mausoleum—lovingly called 'Quaid-e-Azam Ka Mazar' by us, kids—could be viewed for at least five kilometres unobstructed. A decade later, this law would begin to be ignored, and these majestic views would give way to greed and urban decay.

We were part of a little gang called the Daggers Group. Sheldon D'souza, the smartest kid on our street, formed it.

The parking lot behind Faria Apartment was our hideout and playground. This was a long stretch of concrete that we thought our parents never checked, a place where we'd discover new words we weren't supposed to say, form childhood love, and pretend to be gang members.

In between all that, we would play hide and seek, 'running catching', and cricket. The smell of stale, dripping car oil, dust, food being cooked in the apartments above, and chai being brewed would be lost on us as our adrenaline would flow crazily while we ignored our mothers calling us home.

We didn't know much back then, but we did know that while Faria Apartments was generally known as 'that Catholic building', it could also boast of being 'the Christmas building'.

A lot of Pakistanis didn't know what Advent was. As children, we didn't either. Of course, we learned about Advent in Bible class, but only in a cursory way, as we only wanted to pass our exams. Back then, Advent was exciting for us, for reasons that had nothing to do with religion.

Advent, or the beginning of Christmas as far as we cared, meant joining Mum on trips to Saddar to buy Christmas clothes, or joining the children's choir at St Lawrence's Church where we would learn carols that were easy to learn and sing.

As Advent approached, we would be sent out every Friday evening to each of the buildings where Catholics lived and would sing at their doorsteps. Neighbouring Cincinnatus Town was a diverse town, filled with Catholics, Protestants, Shias, Sunnis, Hindus and Parsis. It was also home to large communities of Goans, Tamils, Sinhalese, Mangaloreans and Malabar immigrants, as well as Gujratis and the ethnic indigenous Sindhis.

Many home communities that consisted of villas or apartment blocks regularly hosted only one type of community, not out of malice or segregation, but to ensure the children grew up familiar with the traditions and cultures of Pakistan, Sind, and Karachi, as well as the ethnic cultures inherent to each community. Thus, Faria Apartments, Sherazi Palace and Al Hadi were commonly known as Catholic buildings.

The act of singing from door to door was mostly for charity. We hoped to raise money for the upcoming Christmas fete. Kids singing hoped to get candy and Christmas sweets, but not me. I wanted money.

There was a Casio knock-off digital watch I had seen in the store down the street that cost Rs25. My pocket money was Rs5 per day, and I'd spend Rs3 on Pepsi and Slims. Saving the Rs2 was fine, but I was impatient. That's why I sang. Anyway, singing also meant I could hang around Evelyn, my childhood crush who lived on the floor beneath our apartment.

Everyone in the building thought Evelyn and I would end up marrying each other and living together forever. Well, everyone except Evelyn and me, who were still just growing up. We were infatuated, but never went beyond that. We had so many other dreams we wanted to make real; we just wanted to think we knew what love was.

The singing, writing, Christmas Cards and preparing for Christmas Midnight Mass that was still four weeks away was great, but the only thing we really cared about as kids was the day Mum would say the magic words: Christmas sweets.

Every Catholic family made Pakistani Christmas sweets. And every Catholic family's kids – like my friends and I—loved being part of the making process. The nayori (little puffs stuffed with sweetened coconut shavings and pistachio), the kalkals (one-inch nibbles of deep-fried sweet dough), the toffee (triangular sweets that looked like kaju kattlis but were made of caramel and brown sugar) and the legendary rose cookies. Yes, we were sweet people.

We didn't love helping Mum make sweets because of Christmas, though. We loved helping her make them because we got to eat the leftover pieces of toffee that were too small to bake, or the sweet, uncooked dough that had lumps in them. There was also the most prized reward for our hard work: leftover condensed milk. Mum would pour a teaspoon full straight out of the almost empty can into each of our open mouths, with our tongues sticking out in anticipation.

Advent in Pakistan always meant home to me. It was when Mum and our neighbours' mothers would get together, and it almost always meant good food and a little bit of sugary goodness for us, kids.

It also meant it was time for the Christmas Star.

Every culture has its outdoor holiday decorations. Christians have the star. For us, putting up Christmas stars began the moment the first star was seen on another balcony. We depended on each other in this way; no one ever really knew when to put one up.

Today, all sorts of clever and creative stars are available, from the cheaper foldable ones at the local supermarket to the expensive, bigger and electronic versions that come with multi-coloured bulbs, and sometimes, even tiny speakers playing single-tone carols.

I remember our first Christmas Star. We didn't have much money, but we always wanted Christmas to be special. Mum took us to the market behind our house near the Ismaili Jamaat Khana.

Going to the Jamaat Khana area was always a highlight. A predominantly Ismaili neighbourhood, the entire stretch was a foodie's delight. It could boast of everything from pakora, samosa dhabas and cheap Pakistani burger joints to a branch of the legendary ice-cream chain 'Baloch Ice Cream'. The crown jewel of the area was Thali Land, our own little slice of Indian snack food.

Walking down Jamaat Khana's street all I could see was food, all I could smell were spices and ghee and dosas and all my sister could do was drool while looking at Baloch Ice Cream serving Peshawari scoops.

In the midst of all this culinary goodness and diabetic naughtiness, there was the Garden Store—a local gift shop.

Gift shops were Karachi's version of the Dollar Store—a shop no larger than a typical living room but stocked with every random indulgence buy. Giftshops carried cheap Chinese toys, outlandishly coloured stationery, music, party hats and masks for kids, lots of cheap and popular perfumes like Cachet and Joyous, and every Karachiite's favourite scent: Jovan Musk. Standing in a gift shop, one could be forgiven for thinking they'd consumed LSD; such was the vibrant surroundings and nauseating variety.

Mum loved the gift shop because it had everything that would satisfy Sue and my childish needs, and at Christmas, that need was the Christmas Star.

Our neighbours had put up theirs already. Since our apartment was the corner apartment everyone saw first when turning the street, we had to have the star as well! We walked into Garden Store and right in front of us, hanging from the false ceiling, was a five-pointed star made of short bamboo sticks; the holes between the sticks were covered in kite paper. In the centre of the start, the shopkeeper had hung a small bulb, and my little mind was blown because the dim bulb was flickering, just like a real star.

"Mama, Mama!" I yelled, but she already knew we wanted this one. It was bright red and had small holes which allowed white light to shine through the red hue it threw up. Negotiations followed, which I never really understood, and still struggle with when I shop today. What was originally Rs100, he sold to Mum for Rs40.

The walk home was lighter than we thought. We hung the star from a broomstick we stuck out the kitchen window, with a wire leading in. We did it!

Little did we know that our sweet little Christmas Star would soon be overshadowed by one of the most exciting things that had happened to us in Faria Apartments: the creation of a giant Christmas Star that measured 30 feet high, to be seen from up to eight kilometres away.

The story of our oversized Christmas star is incomplete without the story of Uncle Ronnie.

One evening, while the Daggers Group were playing in the compound, Uncle Ronnie drove a pickup truck into Faria Apartments. Long sticks of bamboo jutted out of the vehicle. We ran after the truck because, quite frankly, besides the tamboos—outsized canopies used in outdoor weddings and fun fairs—we'd never actually seen such large pieces of bamboo up close.

Uncle Ronnie was our favourite family friend. He died when we were still in our early teens, so my only memories of him were as a child and a shy teenager. The earliest memory was because of my sister, Sue. One evening, on Sue's seventh birthday, Mum gave us some money to go downstairs to the store and buy whatever we wanted.

Uncle Ronnie was coming upstairs to our house and saw us. "Where are you rushing off to?"

"It's my birthday!" Sue screamed with unbridled joy.

His face took on the same large grin she showed off, and he said, "Beta, whatever comes out of my pocket, it's yours."

He reached in and brought out Rs.150. Our pocket money was never more than Rs. 5. I immediately told her that she had to share it with me.

We never knew much about Uncle Ronnie other than what we heard others say. But what we did know was that he loved us, he loved motorcycles, and he loved being the centre of the party. We loved these things about him.

It broke our hearts when we heard one day that, in a state of drunkenness, Uncle Ronnie stepped onto the balcony ledge of his fifth-floor apartment and walked into the air. Down he fell, five stories to the ground.

What followed was nothing short of a superhero story.

My best friend, Bubloo, had been standing on the roof of the residence in front of ours and he'd seen the whole thing. What Bubloo also saw was that, after hitting the ground with a sickening crunch, Uncle Ronnie sat up and looked around, delirious, but seemingly unhurt. Afterwards came the wailing. All this happened in a matter of five seconds, from the step, to the drop, to the scream, to doors opening and dozens of footsteps thundering through both buildings.

I had been reading in my room when Mum ran in and told me to take care of Sue because she was running to make sure Uncle Ronnie's family was okay, and to ensure her best friend, Aunty Julie, who was Ronnie's sister, didn't need anything.

I was dying to know what happened, but Mum insisted that I stay in my room with Sue who was asleep in her bed. "Watch TV," Mum said.

As it would turn out, Uncle Ronnie broke almost every bone in his body, but he survived with no life-threatening injuries. I saw him two days later, arriving home from OMI Trauma Centre in a full body cast, with holes in his head cast for eyes, nose and mouth. I wasn't afraid; instead, I was curious about two things: what would he eat and how he would pee.

When they took the cast off and he walked around like nothing had happened, it was as if he knew he'd been given a second chance at life, and he took that seriously. An already larger-than-life man now had no fear of death or consequences and proceeded to live accordingly.

It was this Uncle Ronnie who we chased in his pickup truck that evening. He parked in the corner at the end of the building, near our not-so-secret gang hideout. He jumped out, and whistled loudly, the way grown truckers whistle when calling their friends. Uncle Terrence popped his head out the first-floor window and they nodded at each other, with him rushing down. Together, they pulled out and stacked all the bamboo while we all gathered around, forgetting our games and our cricket balls, as our mothers yelled for us to come home.

We had no idea what was happening, but slowly we realised one word was being repeated by the elders—star. And then it hit me—they were making a star bigger than the one outside my kitchen window.

What followed for the whole week was something that would repeat for the next six years. It was also a memory I'd only revisit once I'd left the country and lived in Dubai for a decade. See, the star of Faria Apartments began as a Christian story.

Uncle Ronnie wanted to build the biggest Christian star in Pakistan, 40 feet high and four feet deep. It would hang from the middle of our two buildings, 100 feet in the air, seen eight kilometres away from the windows of Habib Bank Plaza, Pakistan's tallest tower back then.

It is a Christian story because of what happened the next day. Mum came into our room and told us to get ready to go downstairs with her, to make sure we didn't get in the way of the adults. We leapt to get washed and ready. We had a feeling it had something to do with the star.

As we left our apartment, Evelyn's family met us in the stairwell. We, the kids, were all excited and raring to go. We realised everyone else was leaving their homes too—the newly married couple in apartment 1A, the elderly retired couple in 14A, the Italian missionaries in 22B, the one Muslim family in 28B, the Hindu family in 6C... everyone.

Apparently, Uncle Terrence had posted on the building notice board for Faria families to come join the star-making attempt at 7pm, after daily evening Mass. Sure enough, 30 families had made their way to the back of the building where, to my surprise and excitement, Bubloo and his older sisters were also standing, along with families from the other building.

Uncle Ronnie began by telling us—well, probably telling the elders, but I wanted to believe he meant us, kids, too—what the plan was going to be. The men would use sharp axes to strip the bamboo shoots into thinner trussing, and then tie those sticks together to form a star shape. The women would need to help in sewing swathes of thin red cloth to the bamboo, to flesh out the star between its skeletal structure.

And so, it began. While Mum and some of the other younger women set up their Singer sewing machines on the ground, in a circle, the older women went home and started to brew tea—lots of tea.

The men who weren't involved in the star's construction realised we all needed to eat. There were easily over one hundred and fifty people, including children who would be down there all night. And so, somehow three barbeque pits appeared standing in a row against the wall, with skewers of marinated chicken and beef cubes, and the aroma of coal-fired grilled meat surrounding us.

Thus began the Christmas story of Faria Apartments. Today, I wonder why we ever stopped making that star.

Was it the spirit of Uncle Ronnie that kept it going, and did we stop because he passed away? He died when I was fifteen. Was it because most of the families migrated to other countries and no one from the original story remained? Or was it just the inevitable passage of time and generations who weren't a part of the original story, prompting me to write this, so that the world would know of this little apartment building in Pakistan and its forty-foot star?

Dad used to talk about that star. He'd come down to Karachi from Saudi for Christmas, but he arrived only after it was raised into the sky. Imagine walking into your building after a whole year and seeing that up there, lighting the entire place up. Mum still remembers those evenings fondly. She'd be joined by her two best friends, Aunty Julie and Aunty Jackie, and they'd sew together.

Today, I wonder how it was all financed. Even in the 1980s, Garden East in Karachi wasn't a cheap place to live. Also, most Christians in our building didn't have high-paying jobs, including Uncle Ronnie. How did he finance it? How did the meat for the barbeque suddenly appear and how was it enough for so many of us? How did the tea always taste so good despite dozens of different women brewing it their own way?

Most of all, I wonder if this unbelievable Christmas story, so unique to Pakistan, will ever be told beyond these pages: a story of 50 families, Hindus and Muslims and Parsis and Christians, coming together to showcase what made Karachi great.

Chapter Four

Hot Cross Buns

"If baking is any labour at all, it's a labour of love. A love that gets passed from generation to generation."
- Regina Brett

Hot Cross Buns and a Bohra Muslim Bazaar—funny combination, those two. Yet, every year, Mum made sure we woke up at 5am to buy them. The heart of Saddar in Karachi was host to the oldest Goan Catholic community in Pakistan and the seat of the St Patrick's Cathedral, a British-era centre of Christianity in this vast Muslim city.

Towering over all the other buildings in the vicinity, St Patrick's was a place of wonder. From the majestic Christ the King Monument that greets you when you enter the wide iron gates, to the immense grounds that host a Catholic nursery, sports area, Marian grotto—tomb of an ex-Cardinal—the offices of the Bishop, and the glorious structure itself, the Cathedral and its grounds are home to Catholics across the city.

The Cathedral itself was a work of art, with large yellow stone bricks forming its façade, and gloriously stained glasses adorning the building and casting a kaleidoscope of colours inside, during the day. Inside, it hosted a pulpit for lecters rising up from the floor via spiral stairs to a place higher than the congregation, a feature harkening to the days of the great cathedrals of Europe when microphones didn't exist, and a higher speaking point ensured one reached all ears, no matter how far.

As with all parishes in Karachi, and the world, the Catholic community formed around St Patrick's, with families who had either migrated from Goa, Mangalore and Tamil Nadu, or had already been living there. These families had names like Almeida, D'Souza, Francis, Coutinho, David, Fonseca and Noronha all came there, and soon, a thriving business community established itself. This community lasted for over a century. No name, however, evokes the same reaction as one other—Misquita.

It was Friday; I was 7 years old and Fridays were the days we slept in. I was woken up by Mum to go get Hot Cross Buns; I didn't know any of this. All I knew was that it was 5am, and I was still sleepy.

"Get up," Mum yelled. "It's Good Friday; we're going to get buns." I didn't understand Good Friday, but I do remember the buns.

We were going to Misquita Bakery.

Mum made us sleep early that Maundy Thursday night. We had returned from the first of the Holy Week Masses memorialising when Jesus washed His disciples' feet as a gesture of servanthood. Or as I recall it, those old men with smelly feet getting a foot wash, while the entire church watched. Weird. I'd get the heebie jeebies if someone I didn't know washed my feet.

I didn't mind sleeping early though, because Thursday night meant eating halwa puri from the uncle at Soldier Bazaar the next morning. He packed extra halwa for Sue and me whenever he saw us. He had two kids the same ages as us, and he wanted us to get fat and happy too. In his store, he constantly played music by an artist named Alamgir, as per what Mum mentioned. Doesn't he get tired of listening to the same guy?

Now that I was awake, it was my job to wake Sue up. Sometimes, I'd have to get a glass of water and throw it in her face. 'Like a dead body,' is how our mother described Sue's sleepy state.

Uncle Eddie was waiting outside and as we rushed out, I noticed it was still dark. I remember asking where the sun was. The aroma hit as soon as we turned the corner at Our Lady of Fatima parish and it seemed impossible, as the bakery was still 1.5 kilometres away.

But they had been baking thousands of buns all night, which was why the entire downtown area became thick with the aroma of warm cinnamon and buttery dough.

As we neared the centre of Saddar, I looked around and on that particular day, I saw the area in a new light. I had been too young to notice this, but today, I could see in the silence and the early rays of the dawn, the one hundred and fifty-year-old homes, buildings and shops. Some older than St Patrick's itself.

Made of stone, they looked like they were built yesterday, standing tall and proud. Metal grills framed the balconies, and gas lights hung from some of their porches and entrances.

We finally turned onto Daudpota Road, which along with Clarke Street, was the main artery of the Catholic Community, leading straight to the gates of the Cathedral.

The aroma hit stronger, but I noticed something else—dozens of cars, and hundreds of people, all queueing towards the entrance of Misquita Bakery.

The bakery had been around since 1939 as per Uncle Eddie. He remembered it as a young man, when Mr J.C. Misquita used to run it. After he died, his wife took over, but she wasn't healthy enough to manage it.

"Your Dad loved Misquita Bakery," recalled Uncle Eddie. "Not because of their wares, but because it was a landmark for him when he practised running in Saddar. He would count his kilometres based on where he was in relation to Misquita Bakery and Misquita Blocks, the apartment complex opposite."

Uncle Eddie continued his story. "An ex-employee who used to work there took over with the Misquita family's permission and they moved it closer here to Saddar, and despite being a Muslim, he had been making Hot Cross Buns for us, Catholics in the city for decades."

I loved Uncle Eddie's stories, but there was a particular one which was really interesting for me.

As I child, I never understood the difference between Muslims and Catholics because all my friends in school were just like me. As far as I knew, they had holidays on Christmas, and we got holidays during Eid.

Dad, however, sometimes sounded sad—but mostly angry and nostalgic—when he spoke about this part of Saddar and St Patrick's. He often lamented about the glory days of the suburb, with inter-religious harmony being the beating heart of Karachi's culture. Saddar, St Patrick's, Bohri Bazaar, Empress Market, Misquita Blocks, Lucky Star, and the cinemas all catered to anyone who was in Karachi.

"They didn't care about Muslims, Christians, Hindus and Parsis because no one bothered about differences," Dad would say.

Uncle Eddie told us more about the area. But I already knew what he was going to tell me because Dad told me the same story the year before: The legendary Christ the King Parade of Karachi.

"Every year," he said, "Catholics across Karachi would gather at the start of the street, across the other end from St Patrick's. Bishops from all over Sindh came along with almost every priest in the city."

Altar servers were located at the front, forming the start of the parade, holding up the Cross of Christ high above everyone. The boys behind them would hold the large Bible that is usually held aloft in processions, the flag of the Cathedral and the Church, and they'd march slowly towards the Cathedral in a solemn but excited mood.

"It was as if the soul of Karachi was marching towards its Creator," is how my father described it.

Behind them were the deacons, new students of the priesthood from Karachi's seminary, and then the priests. The priests would be decked out in the finest vestments—bright white in colour.

After the priests came the Bishops, who looked like princes. I recall asking Uncle Eddie why they looked like princes, and he clarified that they were not like princes in fairy tales but princes of the Church, because Christ is their king.

The bishops' attire consisted of bright white and gold vestments, and they held large, golden shepherd-like staffs. I looked confused and Uncle Eddie told me the staffs are curved at the top so that shepherds could use them to pull sheep to themselves. Why would a Bishop need a staff like that? I had never seen sheep in church, except at Our Lady of Fatima parish. Those weren't even real sheep; they were fake and stood in the garden next to Mother Mary's statue.

'Jesus is our Shepherd'. I didn't understand that either. Why is Jesus a shepherd?

Isn't he a king? That's what Uncle just told me. I started to get bored, and he noticed it. So, he shifted back to something more interesting.

The crowd gathered behind the bishops, forming a line to walk together. They joyfully sang hymns praising Christ the King, their voices echoing with 'Hallelujahs' and 'Amens'. Occasionally, the St Patrick's School marching band would take the lead in the procession.

Balconies on both sides of the street proudly displayed large white banners proclaiming Christ Is King, while others had white flags hanging beneath them. People in the balconies joined in the singing, adding to the festive atmosphere of the event.

As the parade continued, people thronged on the rooftops all the way to the Cathedral, showering the parade with flowers like jasmine, roses and others. Sometimes, people would line the streets under the parading feet with palm leaves, reminding everyone of how the people of Jerusalem lined the street when Jesus entered the city on a donkey.

All I remembered about that story was how funny Jesus must have looked while riding a smalln donkey. This particular Easter, Uncle Eddie got emotional. I asked him what was wrong, and he told me that he missed those days. "Where do Christians have this freedom today?" he quietly muttered under his breath.

I saw my Mum return with two large bags smelling divinely of hot cross buns. One bag was for Uncle Eddie's family and one for us. "Why are you crying, Eddie Dada?" I asked. Mum turned to him, surprised, as she noticed the tears. She thought that Sue and I had upset him. She was about to yell at us before he stopped her.

"Things have changed, Son. For fifteen years now, we can't do any of this anymore. Anything that doesn't align with the Muslim faith isn't allowed. It's as simple as that. Your dad knows what I'm talking about. He went through it when he used to run for the country. 'Too much Islam on the tracks and not enough coaching,' he used to tell me."

I had so many more questions, especially now that he mentioned Dad, but he didn't seem like he wanted to share anymore. Mum didn't bother him either and just said, "Let's go home, Dada."

It was quite astonishing when we left, as there were still people in the line who had been there even before we arrived. However, my Mum informed me that she had a connection with someone in the queue. She had called them the day before to ensure that they would purchase tickets for us if they reached the front before us. My Mum was really smart.

On our way back, we decided to make a quick stop at United Bakery because I had been craving their delicious lemon tarts. Little did we know it would turn out to be a bad idea. As soon as we walked in, we bumped into some of Dad's acquaintances, and Mum got caught up in a lengthy conversation with them. Sue and I found ourselves waiting in a corner, feeling hungry and wondering why adults tend to chat endlessly about trivial matters.

Upon finally arriving home, Mum started brewing some tea when the doorbell rang. It was Baba Mama, my Mum's brother. I always found it amusing that they called him that, considering his real name is Augustine, which I find lovely.

Baba Mama came along with my grandma, grandpa, and a few unfamiliar faces. While Sue and I played, one of the unknown individuals went into the kitchen to assist Mum. Mum lightly toasted the buns and spread butter on them, making them smell even more delightful. Then, she began preparing my absolute favourite breakfast: French toast.

No one makes French toast like my Mum. She never makes it dry; she always leaves the centre moist because I once told her that I like it that way.

HOT CROSS BUNS

Everyone got ready for breakfast, and before long, all the buns and French toast were gone. I didn't know why Baba Mama ate my French toast, but I'm glad he did because I was already full.

When Mum reminded us to take a nap before heading out for Good Friday Mass at 2pm, I got a bit annoyed because I didn't like attending the afternoon service in the scorching sun, at 3pm. I'd much rather be home by 4pm to watch the cartoons on PTV. Despite my reluctance, Mum insisted that we rest, so we reluctantly complied.

Why do adults always urge us to sleep, only to wake us up just when we're getting comfortable? I was in a deep slumber when Mum woke me up, but it felt like I had barely closed my eyes for five minutes.

"Wake up, we have to record something for Dad before Mass," she said. Now she had my attention.

I sprang out of bed and quickly freshened up, eager to start the day feeling alert and rejuvenated. At the time, we didn't have a telephone at home, as the phone company hadn't installed the necessary wires in our building. The only way we could communicate with Dad while he was in Saudi was by sending him recordings of our voices, and he would reply by sending us recordings in return. It felt like exchanging letters, but with the sound of our voices. We used small cassettes similar to the ones we used for playing music on our National cassette player. Mum got us ready, ensured the windows and doors were shut to block out any external noise, and pressed play on the last cassette Dad had sent with a friend.

"Hello Beta", I could hear Dad's voice as if he was sitting right next to me. I remember crying because I missed him a bit. He continued to talk about his life in Saudi over the past month and how he had been busy at work. He also told us about the new toy shops that have opened in my favourite mall there. Some of his statements were directed at Mum, so Sue and I couldn't understand a lot of them.

Too much grown-up chatter! I recall seeing Mum tear up. I knew she missed Dad. After listening to the entire message, Mum flipped the cassette around and pressed record.

"Talk."

Somehow, I forgot that we were only recording, and I said 'Hello, Dad?" expecting him to respond. After a couple of hellos, I remembered we were sending him a message and I started to speak about school and the Hot Cross Buns we ate in the morning. I also proceeded to tell him about how I hurt my knees when I fell in the previous week, running in a race in school. I believed he'd be proud of me running just like he did.

Sue was so young, and her voice was really soft, so Mum had to tell her to speak up. She didn't understand how to adjust her volume, so she'd start to yell into the recorder and Mum would laugh. Sue finished telling Dad everything she wanted to say. It was time to go for Mass, so we all said "I love you" to Dad, which was my favourite part of the recordings.

We had to walk to Church because they didn't allow cars for Good Friday Masses. That way, the church compound would be free for the crowd to sit or stand if more people came in.

The Mass was held in the St Lawrence's Boy's School compound, where a large tambu (tent) had been erected. We found a place near the back, where there were still seats available. There were hundreds of people there. I looked for my friends and saw them with their parents in other areas of the grounds. The choir microphone was being tested by the choirmaster and Mr Peter was on stage testing the mic that would be used for the Gospels.

Good Friday Masses were too long and too hot. I didn't know why. Sunday Masses were always one hour long, and they had the same format, so why did we need to sit for 2 hours outside? Mum said it was so that we could feel the pain Jesus felt for us when He was on the Cross, but I didn't understand what that meant. I loved Jesus, but I didn't think He wanted children to sit in the hot sun, listening to boring adults talk about Romans.

The church service began, and we followed along until we reached the Gospel reading. At St Lawrence's, it was tradition for different individuals to recite the Good Friday Gospels. The Priest would take on the role of Jesus, while other men would recite the lines of the Apostles, Pontius Pilate, and others. However, there was a slight issue—they didn't actually recite anything. Instead, they lip-synced to an audio recording from the movie Jesus of Nazareth. Sue and I would always try to stifle our laughter when the older men on stage didn't sync their lip movements correctly, causing their mouths to move after the audio had finished.

Finally, Mass came to an end, and I found myself sweating. Luckily, my Mum was taking us to our Aunt Dorothy's house next door, where we could enjoy some tea and cakes, and relax in a cool room.

As we sat there for the rest of the evening, my mind wandered back to what Uncle Eddie had hinted at earlier. My Dad rarely spoke about why he had stopped running. Most days, he would simply say that athletes grow old like everyone else and eventually lose the desire to run. But there were moments when he would completely avoid the topic, muttering something about managers and their tendency to bring religion into sports. It left me wondering about the true reason behind his decision.

So, I left it at that, too.

Chapter Five

Could You Please Turn to the Friendship Channel?

> "So many people are busy working now, but we need to go back to the old days when grandma and the neighbours helped raise the children, and we were all the better for it." - Kym Whitley

I was five years old, and Sue was three when Mum told us that we were moving into our own home. Not Nana's, Nyena's or Amma's. Ours!

In the year 1985, my family and I were thrilled at the prospect of having a spacious house to call our own. Mum explained to us that this wonderful place was called Faria Apartments. She shared the fascinating story of how the Church had initiated its construction even before I came into this world, acquiring the land and meticulously laying the foundations. It was truly a dream come true for us, and we eagerly anticipated the possibility of having our own rooms if we behaved well and diligently completed our homework.

The Diocese of Karachi wanted it to be a new home for Catholics in the parish devoted to St Lawrence. They finally completed the building in 1985, and we were one of the first to move in.

As we rode to the building, Mum excitedly told us that the building had a total of thirty apartments, some featuring two bedrooms, while others had three. Curiously, I inquired about the number of bedrooms in our unit, to which she chuckled and confirmed it was three. She mentioned that this was why she could promise us our own rooms in the future. Divided into three blocks, each block consists of ten apartments. Our unit was located in Block A, positioned right at the top of the fourth-floor corner. I felt annoyed about being so high up, knowing we would have to climb all those stairs every time we returned home.

That changed once we entered the home. Sue and I ran throughout the place, it looked massive. At least ten times bigger than Amma's home and twice the size of Nana's home. But then, I was tiny, so it was probably just big to me. I didn't care, though. There was enough space for Sue and me to play all our games without worrying about running out of room. We could even invite our friends once we made some.

Sue called me to look at something outside the window. I remember feeling awestruck. All around us, below our line of sight, were thousands of trees lining the streets of Garden East, from palm trees to neem trees and trees whose names I didn't know. Below each of them were rows of beauganvillas, and smaller jasmine and mango trees, filling the air with freshness whenever I took a deep breath.

I could also see, just a slight distance away, the tomb of Muhammad Ali Jinnah, the founder of Pakistan. I remember seeing the tomb when we used to pass by it in a car, but I'd never seen it at this height. Because there were no other buildings between Faria Apartments and the tomb, I could even see the massive doors to the entrance. Mum told me it was about five kilometres away. I didn't know how far that was, but I knew that it took us ten minutes to get there in a car. 'But it's so close, Mama!'

I looked to the right, and there, in the distance, I could see a mighty tower rising above the city, far away. That was the Habib Bank Plaza—the tallest building in Pakistan.

I remember the Plaza. We had gone there on the 14th of August to celebrate Independence Day and see the lights. The tower was lit up, and I thought the architecture was weird. The building had a circular design, with wedges that intertwined with each other. My grandfather, Nyena, explained to me that it was meant to resemble a towering pile of coins, with the wedges mimicking the edges of a coin. From our home in Faria Apartments, I could now see the Plaza any time I wanted to, by just coming to the window!

Taj Court, the only other building of that height in our block was in front of us. It also had four floors, but it had two blocks which meant that it had twenty apartments. I could see people on the balcony, and I immediately noticed some children who were my age. I thought that I'd be friends with them. One of them had a radio-controlled race car. I always wanted one, but we couldn't afford it. I hoped that he'd let me play with his.

Mum pointed out to the left and asked if I noticed anything red on the horizon. As I peered closely, I saw a minaret made of brownstone with a bright red dome at the top, rising into the sky. I could also see the top of a large red dome next to it. "That's St Lawrence's Catholic Church," Mum said, "and that's where we will go for Mass from now on. It's also where you'll go to school; they have a nice one for you and Sue."

St Lawrence's Church turned out to be a two-minute walk from our home; Mum said it was two minutes. It felt like twenty minutes to me. She walked much faster than I could; her legs were longer. I noticed a big mosque on our way to church. Mum told me was called Pakola Masjid. I was surprised because Pakola was the name of my favourite drink. Why is a mosque named after a cola?

Mum told me to shut up and prepare my mind for Mass. She'd tell me everything later. How on earth could I prepare for Mass now that there was a cola mosque near my home?

Once we got home from Mass, I noticed some of Dad's friends waiting for us. Uncle Francis Rodrigues, my godfather, his brother, Menin, and our ground floor neighbour—Uncle Eddie Francis. I liked all of them because they were fun to be with, and they always told me wonderful stories.

That night was no different. Mum told Uncle Menin and Uncle Eddie about my questions, and they immediately started to inundate me with the history of Garden East.

They told me about Soldier Bazaar, a traditionally Catholic area which is one of the oldest suburbs in Karachi. It was close to an older district called Cincinnatus Town. Soldier Bazaar was one of the most politically important districts in all of Pakistan.

Soldier Bazaar was the residence of GM Syed, a prominent figure in the Pakistan Movement in Sindh. His home, known as Hyder Manzil, was constructed in 1932. Interestingly, Hyder Manzil was frequently visited by Muhammad Ali Jinnah, the founder of Pakistan, as well as our first Prime Minister, Liaquat Ali Khan. These names hold significance for me as they were also the names of our Group Houses in school: Jinnah House, Liaquat House, Iqbal House (named after Allama Iqbal, our national poet), and Latif House.

"Did you know the Pakistan Resolution was written right here in Soldier Bazaar in 1943?" Uncle Eddie asked me. At age five, I didn't even know what a resolution was. But I nodded because I didn't want to seem uneducated. These uncles are so cool, and I wanted to look cool as well.

"There's a zoo next door," I yelled out in excitement. Sue's ears perked up, clearly bored with our conversation. To my delight, I was informed about Gandhi Garden, which is now known as Karachi Zoo, just a couple of streets away from our house. They led me to the back balcony and directed my attention to a gate that was barely visible amidst the dense foliage of the surrounding trees. In Garden East, it was against the law to construct anything taller than four stories, to ensure the safety of the numerous bird species in the area.

I couldn't hold in my excitement. A zoo right next to our house! Just then, I heard a low rumble and Uncle Eddie informed me that it was the lions roaring, signalling that sunset was close. He was right, I could hear that same roar every evening coming from that direction. The night was filled with fascinating stories, and I learned so much. However, they still hadn't answered my question about the mosque. They instead began to tell me about the street we lived on, Manekjee Street.

Manekjee Dastoor Dhala, a notable figure in Pakistan during the 19th and 20th centuries, was named after one of the most prominent Parsis of his time (Zoroastrians). According to Uncle Eddie, he was widely recognized but not particularly liked by his own community. In contrast to the typical humble, quiet, and diplomatic nature of the Parsis, Manekjee stood out for his outspoken and blunt demeanour, which was not well-received by those who preferred a more agreeable lifestyle within the community.

I also discovered that Manekjee had travelled to the United States to study at Columbia University, and was supported financially to do so by none other than the renowned Indian business family, the Tata Group. The street was named after him in honour of his position as the only High Priest of Zoroastrianism in Karachi—one of the last major strongholds of the Parsis in the sub-continent outside Bombay.

Due to the street's prominence, numerous influential families relocated there, representing a diverse range of religions. At the beginning of Manekjee Street, the first villa served as the residence of the Al Karam Textiles family, the nation's largest textile company. Across from them resided the Pakola family, renowned for founding Pakistan's most beloved soda. The Pakola family contributed both land and money towards the construction of the Ghafooria Mosque, which was later nicknamed Pakola Masjid because of them.

Behind Faria Apartments was the Igloo Ice Cream family, which Mum told me was Pakistan's most popular ice cream brand. A few villas away lived the lawyer of a popular politician, Mian Muhammad Nawaz Sharif, whom I didn't know at the time would go on to become the prime minister of the country.

Manekjee Street also branched out towards the inner suburbs that made Garden East something of an outlier in Karachi. To the left of the street, one lane in, began one of two major Ismaili strongholds. Ismailis are the followers of the sect of Islam led by the Agha Khan. Their place of worship is called a Jamaat Khana (literally, gathering place), and just like Catholic parishes, believers build their homes around it. The one behind our home was lovingly called the Masala Society, which I didn't understand, because masala means spice. The other Ismaili community branched off from the end of the street, which was where the second biggest Jamaat Khana in Karachi was located. It was as large as most European cathedrals and was a true work of architectural beauty. Under the Jamaat Khana was a myriad of 'mom and pop' stores lining the streets, from Indian snacks like dosas and idlis, to homemade Chinese food, greasy delicious burgers and Peshawari ice cream.

Towards the right, the street gave way to Pedro D'Souza Road that led people to St Lawrence's Parish. Taking a left at the end of Pedro D'Souza Road, you would come to Cincinnatus Town, which had one of the largest Shia populations in Pakistan, hosting their place of worship called an Imambargah. Catholics and Shias lived in Cincinnatus town peacefully for decades. It's why the area is lovingly called Catholic Colony, even by the Shias!

"Do you know the names of all the other streets here?" My uncles and aunts asked me. I had no idea. They told me about how Manekjee Street was just one of many amazing names. Garden East was also home to Love Lane, Britto Road, King Street (named after King George), Robin Street, Rose Avenue, Clayton Street, and so many more. My head started spinning as I listened to all the names. It seemed like we were in England, not Pakistan, I told them. Uncle Francis told me it wasn't surprising, since we had many English people resident in Karachi, who did a lot for the city, as well as Goan Catholics who had come from India and stayed here. This was why many streets were named after them.

It was fun knowing about Pakola Masjid, but I didn't really care much about all the other things they told me. I decided to go and check out the house again. We didn't have much furniture—just a bed, a wood sofa set and a small tabletop gas stove. They were all gifts Mum and Dad got for their wedding or for moving into the new home.

Another thing we didn't have was a television set. This was upsetting because we just came back from Saudi Arabia where we'd watch cartoons all day on Dad's TV.

One evening, around 8pm, Mum called Sue and me to the window. She'd put up a stool and told us to stand on it. She pointed to the house across from us in Taj Court, to a balcony on the third floor. The people who lived there had left their balcony door open wide, and their television was facing us. It was a huge television, the biggest I'd ever seen, and the volume was up high.

Mum was excited and I could see why. There was a Pakistani soap opera airing, and she could see and hear it clearly from across the street. We got bored very quickly and ran back inside to play. A few minutes later, we heard Mum talking loudly in Urdu and it wasn't to us.

We ran back to her, curious, and saw her sporting a huge, happy smile. She told us the neighbours looked out and saw her watching their TV; one of them came out onto the balcony to ask if we were the new family who moved in. When Mum said yes, she asked if Mum was watching the soap opera. Mum told her that she was, and the woman went in and turned the volume even higher. She came back out and said that Mum could watch from where she was, or she could come over and watch with them. Mum said she'd come over the next day. She seemed really happy that night and we were happy for her.

The next day, she went to the window at the same time and sure enough, they were watching TV again. We asked her why she didn't go over, and she replied that she didn't know them well enough. Mum was naturally a person.

The lady came out to the balcony again and told Mum that if she didn't come over, she'd close the balcony door and she won't be able to watch anything!

I remember one day when Mum dressed us up in really fancy clothes because she said we were going to someone's home for the first time. I never understood this. Why did we need to impress someone with our clothes? But she made me wear my Gummy Bears tee, so I didn't complain.

We went over to Taj Court, and as we began to climb the stairs, I perceived the aroma of freshly ground spices and burnt oil. It smelled like someone had just cooked something, and I became really hungry. We arrived at the house to meet the door wide open, and the family waiting for us.

The woman emerged from the house to greet us, appearing to be around the same age as my mother. She warmly embraced my mum, introducing herself as Rizwana. She explained that she and my mum are Pukhtoon and Sindhi. As we entered the house, Rizwana introduced us to the rest of the family: Bhabhi, whose real name remains a mystery, as everyone refers to her by that title, Razzak, Rubina, Shahid, Shazia, and Qurat-ul-Ain. We all gathered in the living room to watch a TV show, which Sue and I found uninteresting, as it involved adults discussing topics we didn't care about. However, Bhabhi invited us to join her in another room where we discovered that they also had children. We happily played with them.

Mum now had her first friend, and it all began with a television set and a balcony.

Shortly after, we met all our other neighbours. Mum liked two people in particular. One of them was Aunty Jacqui who was really fashionable and lived in Block C, on the first floor. She always wore the kind of clothes we saw in magazines. The other was Aunty Julie who also lived in Block C, but on the fourth floor, like us.

Faria Apartments was where I and Sue made a lot of friends, particularly because they were all Catholics. While I was an introvert, I quickly befriended a boy named Shane Caldeira, the eldest of six siblings whose family came from Sri Lanka and settled in Karachi. I first experienced the thrill of the Knight Rider series, the excitement of Air Wolf, and the unforgettable theme music of Streethawk at Shane's house.

Sue and I also made friends at Taj Court. I used to believe that everyone I knew was Muslim until the day I met Wayne Turner, a boy who was much shorter than me but had twice the energy. Wayne turned out to be the proud owner of a super-fast race car, and we bonded like chicken tikka and chilled Coke. Wayne then introduced me to Murad, also known as Bubbloo, who happened to be the funniest kid I had ever met. Bubbloo and I quickly became close friends.

As it turned out, Bubbloo was Ismaili and attended the Masala Jamaat Khana. Bubbloo introduced me to Jonathan, who was the nephew of Aunty Julie and lived in the same apartment as her. Jonathan's father was based in the US, so Jonathan resided here while his paperwork was being sorted out.

Jonathan had a unique trait that set him apart from the rest of us—his impressive height. Standing at least 2 feet taller than his peers, he definitely stood out in a crowd. However, what truly caught everyone's attention was not his towering stature, but his luxurious hair. Jonathan's silky locks were the envy of many, always perfectly styled despite their tendency to flop around. It was no secret that his great hair and towering height played a big role in his success with the girls.

Speaking of girls, one day, Mum told us that we were going to visit our newest neighbours. A family had just moved into the apartment under ours, on the third floor.

The D'Souza family was an all-girl family, with their father, Uncle Edward, being the only male in the home. We visited their house with Mum, who brought along a dish she prepared for them. As they brewed tea and chatted, Sue and I engaged with their children. Lorraine, their second daughter, was a pretty and tall girl, whereas Edna, the youngest, was petite, short, and possessed the most captivating eyes I had ever seen on a girl.

Positioned between the two girls was another girl who captivated my attention effortlessly. Evelyn, the eldest daughter. She was about my age and possessed the most beautiful face I had ever seen. We got along instantly and began to frequently visit each other's homes. Everyone began to teasingly refer to Evelyn and me as the new 'couple' in Faria Apartments, which made me wonder who the old couple were.

Aunty Julie and Aunty Jacqui regularly visited us, and we visited them too. Auntie Julie had a brother named Uncle Ronnie who was the tallest man I'd ever seen. He also had an amazing motorcycle—the kind people rode on desert dunes.

I counted the people in each apartment in Faria and Taj. There were one hundred and twenty- seven people in Faria Apartments, and around half of that number in Taj Court.

What I didn't realise until later was that Taj Court had more than just Muslims. There were Shia Muslims, Sunni Muslims, Ismaili Muslims, eight Catholic families and one Hindu family living there. It felt like I was back in the Bangali Parra with so many people from all over Pakistan, but with better rooms.

One day, Uncle Ronnie called everyone in the building on the phone and told them he was organizing a picnic for families in Faria and Taj, and if anyone was interested, they needed to meet him that evening to discuss the whole thing. Mum decided to go because that was how we could make friends with our neighbours.

She returned to tell us that we were all going to a beach called Sand Spit. I found this name funny because I didn't understand why we would want to go to a beach that everyone spits in. I thought that adults were weird.

The day came for us to go for the picnic, and we were sleepy because we stayed up all night with Mum, Aunty Jacqui and her husband, Terrance, who had come over to help make the snacks.

We all helped. Mum asked me to cut the sides off the sandwich bread slices. Sue was told to make sure all the crumbs were quickly swept off the floor, so that we wouldn't get cockroaches.

Uncle Terrance buttered all the bread. Mum made a special green chutney spread that everyone loved, and Aunty Jacqui made corned beef paste. I loved corned beef sandwiches; they were the best. But I loved chutney sandwiches too. I'm not sure which one I'd eat more.

The buses arrived to take us to the beach at 7am. We all went down, and I was caught by surprise. Both apartment compounds were full of people—hundreds of them, some of whom I'd never seen before.

The aroma of tea filled the air— lots of tea. It smelled like the Bangali Parra all over again. Then I saw why. The Francis family were carrying three massive thermoses of the tea Uncle Eddie's wife, Aunty Francine, had just made.

I also saw other families carrying things—Evelyn's mum carried a large pot of biryani. Shane's mum carried boxes of Tupperware, which I could only hope were her famous chicken rolls. They were so good that Father Robbie in St Lawrence's had asked her to sell them in the Church compound after Mass.

All the husbands and men in the buildings carried the bigger pots of curries, fried fish and speakers. Yep, speakers! It wasn't a big Christian Pakistani picnic if you didn't hear the voices of Jim Reeves and the BeeGees filling the air. Sue and I were very excited. We had never been at a picnic this big before, and we'd only ever been to the beach opposite our home in Saudi Arabia.

On the bus, someone said that we should pray, so everyone made the sign of the Cross, and we all said the 'Our Father.' I wonder what the Muslims on the bus thought about that. But I saw some of them also making the sign, although getting it wrong.

"Isn't that sweet?" Mum asked. I nodded, not knowing what that meant.

What I did know, however, was that Bubbloo, Wayne and Jonathan were on the bus too, but were sitting with their families. I couldn't wait for the bus to stop, for us to play. I noticed Wayne reading something. Why would he be reading on a picnic?

The bus finally stopped, but the place didn't look like a beach. It had some roadside market. The men get off the bus and I craned my neck to look out the bus window. It looked like they were buying a trunk of ice and another trunk of cold drinks. Now, I was excited, because I don't really like tea. I wanted Pakola.

They got back on the bus, and we started towards Sand Spit. When we got there, the buses parked on the road, close to two dilapidated huts. Everyone carried something into one of the huts and placed them in the rooms. This was to enable us find things easily.

I could smell the ocean. It smelled saltier than the water in Saudi. But the water seemed rougher too. I could hear waves crashing. All of us, kids, rushed to the front of the hut to look; there were waves higher than us crashing into the beach. Uncle Ronnie turned to Mum and said "Don't let the kids go in yet. We'll have breakfast and then see."

Surely, after breakfast, the water had subsided, and everyone jumped into the sea. It was so salty that I immediately started coughing and rubbing my eyes. This wasn't as exciting as I thought.

I ran back into the hut where Mum was helping in the kitchen. She laughed and told me that this is what sea water was like in Pakistan. I didn't like the saltiness of the water, but at least I had other kids to play with. I wandered into the other huts to find my friends. That was when I noticed the book Wayne was reading, on a table. I picked it up and I realised that there were coloured pictures in it. It looked different, and I started reading the cover. It had a man dressed in green and purple, with an alien-like head. The title was 'Justice League'. I didn't understand what Justice League was, but I was excited because the character on the cover looked like he was fighting Superman.

I sat down in a corner and started to read it. I didn't even realise how much time had passed. I went from page to page, devouring every word and chapter, not knowing who these superheroes were or even whether they were superheroes. I saw people flying in space—one of them carried the sun, and another one made flowers grow out of nothing. I'd never seen anything like this.

I ran to Mum to ask her if I could get a book like this. She agreed and promised to take me to Mangal Bazaar to get one. "It's a comic book", she said. I didn't know what a Mangal Bazaar was or what a comic book was, but I nodded happily and kept the book where I had found it.

As the evening approached, Uncle Eddie started to call everyone back from the water for tea. Bubbloo's family had brought samosas and pakoras for everyone, so we all settled into a sort of siesta. Everyone got a cup of tea and whichever snack they wanted.

We began to hear music blare out of the other hut. Uncle Ronnie was carrying a tape recorder while Jonathan carried the speaker behind him. They placed it on the front porch of the hut facing the sea, and the words, "We Didn't Start the Fire" filled the air. Uncle Terrance told me that the song was recorded by a man called Billy Joel, who was his favourite. Suddenly, Rizwana yelled out to Uncle Ronnie, telling him to put on some Pakistani music, so that the rest of them could enjoy it too. So, he changed the cassette and a song called 'Jogia' started playing.

I was mesmerised. I had only ever heard English rock music because of the stuff Dad and Uncle Jerry used to play. But here was a wonderful song that made me instantly fall in love with it, and it wasn't in English. It was Urdu. Uncle Ronnie saw me and my awestruck face and told me that the song was done by a newly famous band called Junoon, whose lead singer was Fifi Haroon.

I was now in love with Pakistani music, even though I didn't know any Pakistani artiste other than Junoon and Fifi Haroon. I knew all I needed to nag my mum so that she would buy me this song. I heard many other names, like Vital Signs, Milestones and Nazia Hassan. Aunty Cecilia, who is Evelyn's aunt, told me her best friend, Candy, was in Milestones and that she might sing for her wedding. I couldn't wait. Candy's voice reminded me of Joan Jett, one of Uncle Jerry's favourite singers.

While my tastes in music continued to grow, it would be years later, in 1992, that I suddenly discovered a whole new world of Pakistani music as a soon-to-be teenager.

I was in eighth grade and the number one music show on TV was Gold Leaf Rhythm Wythm— a thirty-minute show showcasing the best of new Pakistani music. Bubbloo, Jonathan and I were now obsessed with pop music, especially because of the new audio systems Jonathan and I had.

Uncle Ronnie bought a new Technics deck, which had 5 racks of different audio systems in one and the speakers were bigger than we were. He liked to take a speaker and place it on the balcony, playing Nusrat Fateh Ali Khan's 'Dum Mast Qalandar' or Enigma's 'Sadeness'. I admired him a lot, so I tried to do the same. Dad has recently bought us a 3CD changer by Aiwa, and the speakers were like tiny little bombs, exploding with sound we didn't think was possible.

I played Bryan Adams and Haddaway on the system a lot, and sometimes, I played Junoon, but I became bored with them. I preferred Ali Haider more. In fact, I loved Ali Haider. His album, 'Sandesa' was my favourite album of all time from Pakistan, even though it had been only two years since it was released.

Uncle Ronnie later introduced me to Virgil. Virgil was a record store on Tariq Road, the fancy retail area where we got all our clothes. It was a bit pricey, but because everyone else shopped there, we did too. Right next to the incredible new Dolmen Shopping Centre was a small shop called Virgil Music, which had a fancy logo that looked like something I had seen before.

Two individuals were seated behind the counter, one being the owner and the other the manager, whom everyone called Shankar Bhai. Uncle Ronnie would often acquire his music from this place due to Shankar Bhai's extensive knowledge in the field. However, the cassettes were quite pricey, costing Rs. 75. My mother would advise me to abandon the idea and purchase cassettes from Regal like everyone else, which were priced at Rs. 25. Reluctantly, I agreed to her suggestion, but secretly, I saved up my pocket money each month to purchase a cassette from Virgil.

But why? Because I learnt that they had a massive collection of CDs, old and new, and they recorded the CDs onto TDK cassettes that made them sound amazing. They also made personalised mixtapes for those who wanted them, for the same price. So, every month I'd go to Virgil with a list of 18 different songs and they'd record them from CDs onto a cassette for me.

I was a happy twelve-year-old, as I could now make high-quality mix tapes for Evelyn!

Chapter Six

An Arrow to Your Heart

"Democracy is the best revenge." - Benazir Bhutto

As an 8-year-old, hearing sirens never failed to scare me. I never understood why everyone went home and why mum yelled at us to come upstairs and stop playing. The cars disappeared from the roads and the entire Garden East area went quiet. The only sounds we'd hear were crows at twilight and the faint roar of the lions of Karachi Zoo, a few kilometres away.

Mum told me that it was because of the curfew. Martial Law, Uncle Augustine called it, but I didn't understand what he meant. He told me that it was when the army took over a country to help it become better.

I didn't know how it could become better if no one was outside. But then, I didn't understand much of these things anyway. I believed that adults never really knew what they were doing. They would make decisions about something and then fight about the decision later. For some reason, everyone talked about this man called Zia-something, I couldn't pronounce his last name. He was the person in charge. He ran the country, and according to people on the news, he always flew around the world getting people to help us.

The sirens went off every evening, loud and clear across the city. Mum wasn't happy about it, but she never liked to talk about these things. She never answered our questions because 'it was too dangerous' to talk about. "Don't bring it up with your friends," she'd always say. I didn't like that.

We always went to the church compound to play and catch up with friends. We liked to stay there as long as we could, but we all knew when the sirens were about to go off.

One day, however, I heard someone shouting from another apartment. Mum rushed to the window and saw that it was one of our neighbours. More people came running to their balconies. At the same time, I started hearing the sounds of car horns bellowing around us.

The entire area and the city seemed to be celebrating something. Mum then turned to us and said "I think the curfews will end soon. Zia is dead!"

I didn't realise so many people hated him this much, because it seemed like it was a birthday party instead of the day someone died. I thought we were supposed to be sad for people who died.

A few months passed by quickly, as the city returned to what Mum referred to as 'normal'. Suddenly, I started seeing flags everywhere we went to in Soldier Bazaar—on streetlights, in windows, hanging from balconies and from fences. Some flags were black, red and green, with arrows. They were always in the same area, and alongside them were posters with the photo of a woman with a dopatta on her head. The letters P were on the flags, three times. The arrow was spray-painted along the walls of the buildings and villas of Garden East.

One evening, Mum excitedly opened the door for Aunty Jacqui, Aunty Julie, and Rizwana. They all came into the living room. They seemed really enthusiastic, as they were planning something big. Sue and I sat with them, but we couldn't understand what they were talking about. Something was happening the next morning and they wanted to talk about what they would wear and what they would chant.

"Aunty Julie, why do you want to shout?" Sue asked.

Aunty Julie told us that they would be shouting chants and singing songs as they went to vote. I didn't know what a vote was, but I think it was something big like a party. It had to be a party if everyone was talking about what they were going to wear.

Aunty Jacqui told Mum that they'd leave at a certain time. Mum and Aunty Julie told her that it was too early. Apparently, Mum was known to take too long to get ready, which was why they needed to give her an earlier time. Sue and I laughed because we knew it was true. Mum loved her eyeliner and took her time to do her hair, which was really long and silky. I believed Mum had the longest hair in our entire family.

The next morning, Mum woke up for a quick breakfast. She was ready. She'd done her hair and makeup and was wearing a beautiful green shalwar qameez and dupatta. We heard the sound of commotion downstairs and rushed to the window.

A large number of women gathered in the compound of our two buildings, with more joining them each minute. They were all singing a song I couldn't identify. Someone saw us in the window and yelled that we should tell Mum to come downstairs soon.

We saw our friends with their mothers, and we rushed to tell Mum that we were going down to meet them. Mum's already at the door, waiting for us.

As we all left the building to get to the road, I realised that everyone was walking; there were no people in cars... and they were all women!

The women of the entire area had come out with their kids, and were all walking towards Numaish, the massive roundabout and park near the Quaid's Mausoleum. Our destination was Nishtar Park, the public park near the roundabout. As we walked down Maneckji Street towards Soldier Bazaar, which was the way to Numaish, I noticed gates of villas opening up. The women in the Al Karam Textiles mansion, the Pakola family and more, all started to join our march to the park.

Suddenly, I heard loud music. Someone had brought their car and slowly rode alongside the women, with their speakers playing a familiar song. It was the song I'd heard being sung earlier. It went 'Dila Teer Bija, allay...' and all the women sang along loudly. It was mesmerising; even Sue and I started singing. I asked Mum what the song was, and Rizwana turned to answer, saying it was the Balochi folk song, Dila Teer Bija, which is the anthem of Benazir Bhutto's PPP, or Pakistan People's Party—the political party they were all going to vote for. That was what the three Ps on the posters meant.

I asked Mum who Benazir was, and she pointed to the hundreds of newer posters plastered on the walls of the street we were on and hanging from the streetlamps. She was the woman with a dopatta on her head looking towards the heavens, and a large red, black and green arrow hovering above her head, with PPP in white letters on it.

Benazir Bhutto! The name sounded like a powerful name, and I never forgot it.

I remember singing even louder, but I didn't know what the words meant, so I asked Rizwana's sister, Rubina, who taught me Sindhi. I thought she would know since she understood so many languages.

She quietly told me the meaning in English, as everyone continued their chant.

"Dila Teer Bija means an arrow to your heart, and it's about taking on the enemy and defeating them."

Rizwana piped in to tell me how Benazir Bhutto was the daughter of a previous Prime Minister of Pakistan, and how she was the new hope of the country, and of women everywhere. I didn't understand how any of this mattered, but I could see that everyone thought it was important. After all, the way we were marching seemed like we were in the army, going to battle.

After a while, we reached Nishtar Park, where a large crowd had already gathered before us. Aunty Jacqui heard someone say that they were already waiting hours earlier, so that they could vote in time.

The halwa puri stand was closed too, so I realised that we weren't going to have halwa puri this morning. It didn't matter because Mum packed French toast for us. My favourite!

There was a man on a loudspeaker yelling announcements to everyone, telling the crowd where to queue up and how the women would have a separate section to queue up. There were hundreds of women in front of us in the queue we got into, which suggested that we were going to be here for a long time.

Time passed by quickly though. There were musicians who came to the park to play folk songs as we waited. It seemed like everyone was in a party mood, as if something amazing was about to happen.

Days later, Mum switched on the TV that we had bought a few months ago, to watch the Khabarnama at 9pm. Benazir Bhutto had won something because of our votes and was now Prime Minister of Pakistan. Mum translated the difficult Urdu that the newscaster spoke; she told us that Bhutto was now the youngest female Prime Minister in history, and the first female Prime Minister of a Muslim-majority country.

All of that sounded important to Mum. I could see happiness on her face as she took us to the balcony, where we saw fireworks erupt in the air and heard gunshots, as people celebrated Bhutto's victory. We also heard hundreds, if not thousands, of cars honking again. This time, for longer. I also saw people running into the streets and dancing. Garden East looked very different that night. I was sure all of Pakistan did too.

A few years went by, and Garden East looked even more different now. The flags of the PPP had now been intertwined with another flag, displaying the colours white, red, and green, along with the letters MQM. These flags could be seen proudly waving on poles throughout the southern region of Garden East, guiding the way towards Nishtar Park. Interestingly, it appeared that the right side of the street leading up to the park was adorned with MQM flags, while the left side proudly showcased the flags of the PPP.

I knew this because of my bicycle. My mum thought it was time for me to have a bike to navigate the neighbourhood whenever she needed me to run errands to the market. She didn't want me riding the fancy blue BMX bike that my dad had given me a few years back. "It's bright blue and it looks foreign; I'm sure someone will steal it from you!" she'd always say.

One morning, Mum took me to the bicycle shop that was on the left side of the street, halfway between Faria Apartments and Nishtar Park. Mum was a shrewd negotiator, and they settled on a price. She remarked, "I can't believe you're still charging me this much even after the discount. Why is it so expensive?" The shopkeeper replied, "Dekho

Madam, we have to make our own profit, and we also have to make sure the Party gets its profits, otherwise, we'll be put out of business." Mum slowly nodded as if it dawned on her what he meant.

She explained on the way back home that it seemed the shopkeeper needed to pay bribes to local party leaders to survive. If he made a sale, he had to count not just his own cut and the supplier's cut, but also the local powers that be, else they'd force him to shut down, if not worse. It sounded like something Lex Luthor would do in Metropolis, but I thought Benazir was supposed to be our Superman.

Slowly, in the coming years, it became worse, as Catholics started leaving the area. Many moved to the Cantonment area we all called Cantt. St Anthony's was the go-to parish, as was close to the more affluent Clifton area, and many Catholics in Garden East sold their homes to go live there.

Unfortunately, not a lot of Catholics could afford the high prices of Garden East's older buildings, because the community had maintained the buildings really well. So, owners ended up selling their apartments to non-Catholics, which drove down the community aspect of our Parish. Where every balcony would have a small Christmas star during December, we now saw only two or three.

Years ago, young parishioners from St Lawrence's would walk around to each of the buildings and sing Christmas Carols from the compound, while people would come out to their balconies and join them in singing. At this moment, they were not allowed to do that anymore, as the Muslims in the buildings didn't like that.

Garden East still had many flowers, but not as much as before.

Chapter Seven

The Sacred and the Scared

"Love, friendship and respect do not unite people as much as a common hatred for something." - Anton Chekhov

The year was 1992.

One morning, in school, it was time for our weekly religion class, which was usually conducted by Sister Mary. We loved Sister Mary because she made our faith easier to understand by using real-life examples. That morning, however, was a bit different. As we left the classroom to go to the little room where religion classes were held, Sister Mary stopped us in the corridor and asked those of us who were Catholic boys to join her downstairs, near the principal's office.

We thought we were in trouble. However, we decided to go with her because while she had a sombre look, she also had a firm glint in her eye, as if something interesting was going to happen. As we marched down to the office, she turned to us and said, "You cannot tell anybody about this right now, because it's very sensitive."

As a twelve-year-old, I didn't understand what sensitive meant, but I knew it was something she was serious about. I realized we had to behave like responsible adults. We reached the Principal's office, where he joined Sister Mary to tell us that we were about to go out on an excursion. This was amazing! We had never actually been on a school excursion before.

We asked why none of our other classmates joined us in receiving this information and why we were asked to be quiet about it. Sister Mary said, "This excursion is only for the Catholic boys of the school, from your class and the class below you."

We inquired about our destination, and she mentioned that she would inform us shortly. After a few minutes, a spacious van arrived. Sister Mary joined us in the back of the van instead of sitting in the front with the driver. It became apparent that she was about to reveal the purpose of our journey.

A few days prior, a significant event had taken place in India. Sister Mary turned to us and inquired if we, as boys, were aware of the news or if our parents had informed us about the incident. None of us had much information. Curious, we asked her to explain further.

Sister Mary said, "Well, a couple of days ago, a mob of Hindu extremists stormed an ancient Muslim mosque in India, in a city called Ayodhya. The mosque's name was Babri Masjid, and it was built in the year 1528 by a man named Mir Baqi, a general in Mughal Emperor Babur's empire. We had studied about Emperor Babur in school, so we knew who he was, but we had never studied about Babri Masjid. However, we could now see why it was named after him.

Sister Mary told us about how the Babri Masjid was incredible in its architecture, with renowned Western historians, particularly noting its acoustics. Despite being large in size, one could hear a whisper from one end of the Mosque, at the other end, over 200 feet away.

For some reasons—which we didn't understand as children, because adults could be confusing about these things—politicians and religious leaders in India claimed the Mosque was built on the ruins of a much more ancient Hindu temple. Hence, they declared the land on which the Mosque stood was rightfully theirs, and that it encroached on grounds that are sacred to Hindus.

This happened after years of infighting, causing the land to be disputed for many years. Many politicians on both sides had used this dispute as a means to gather votes and support from their respective voting bases.

"A couple of days ago, things reached a tipping point, resulting in thousands of Hindu men storming the mosque and destroying it, using various means. They didn't care who got hurt in the process." The resulting outrage which ensued enveloped the city itself and many countries in a wave of hate-related violence between Hindus and Muslims, including next door Pakistan.

We were a bit confused as to why Sister Mary was telling us all this. After all, we were Catholic and we were in Pakistan, miles away from India. What did any of this have to do with us?

Hearing this question, Sister Mary's eyes welled up with tears. "Well, a large number of Muslims in Pakistan exist who don't understand that anyone who's not a Muslim isn't necessarily a Hindu and have taken great offence to this act. Across Pakistan, there have been multiple protests and rallies against this destruction, and many of these protests have turned violent. Muslims have led throngs of other Muslims to go and violently attack non-Muslims who they thought were Hindu."

Because of this, in Karachi as well, a mob of thousands of Muslims decided to march up to the Sacred Heart Catholic Church in Kaemari, a suburb of Karachi, near the port where many Hindus and Christians have lived for centuries. The Sacred Heart Church was a mainstay of Christians in the area, serving the congregation which consisted of mostly poor Urdu and Punjabi-peaking converts or migrants. The Church itself was a modest structure, with a beautiful, but simple altar and pews that seated around two hundred believers during Mass and other celebrations.

The mob unleashed their violent rage onto the Church, including the parish priest.

"We are going there now, children, to see just what happens when you practice the love for your religion by showing hatred for another religion, and not the love that your faith actually teaches you. What you're about to see will be very disturbing. I will be with you throughout this, but I want you to understand that we have a choice when we see acts like this. That choice is, we can choose to be hateful against the people who did this or we can forgive them and pray for God to change their minds and hearts. It's easy to choose revenge, anger, or rage. But it's very difficult to choose love, which is what Jesus did on the Cross. When you see what we're about to see, you might feel confused, upset, or concerned, especially given your age. But we don't know how long this will continue and whether there will be any more protests to come. All of us across Pakistan are in danger because of the fundamentalists who are choosing to treat this as a free-for-all. Do not let this change who you are. In fact, let's pray the Rosary and ask Mother Mary to protect us."

We decided to pray the Sorrowful Mysteries on the way there, and somehow, the van became very quiet as we rode towards the Church.

As we got closer, Sister Mary once again turned to us. "Boys, it's okay if you feel angry at what happened. Anger is justified. Anger is a natural human response. Even Jesus, when He entered the temple where the sellers were selling their wares, got angry at them because they were treating the temple badly. Don't let your anger let you take it out on anyone you know who is a Muslim."

The van stopped and parked on the side of the road. We all got out, and Sister Mary and the principal took us towards Sacred Heart Church. The closer we got, the more we realized how bad things were. The gates of the church courtyard had been mangled and looked like people had tried to break it open and had succeeded. In fact, it looked like a car had crashed through it.

The churchyard was filled with scattered debris. There were shattered construction blocks, bricks, and mud from the garden where someone had attempted to uproot and ruin the flowers. As we approached the church building, we noticed that the doors were shattered. Additionally, there were burn marks indicating that someone had made an effort to set the doors ablaze. We entered the church, and our hearts broke.

The ground was scattered with shattered statues of Jesus, Mother Mary, the Sacred Heart statue, St Joseph, and Baby Jesus. It appeared that these statues were not only thrown down to break them, but also stomped on with great force, leaving them completely crushed.

Whoever had done this had committed blasphemy, not just against Christians, but against the teachings that the prophets in their own religion had taught them. All the pews could be seen broken or burned.

The floor was a mess. We shakily started to turn our eyes towards the altar, horrified at the sight. In front of us, the altar was a mess. The table was broken and hacked, and the tablecloth that was blessed by the bishop had been ripped and torn. The podiums where the statues previously stood had been hacked away with axes.

It surprised us that these people had brought axes to a church. What really struck us in that moment of despair and unquenchable sorrow, however, was a sight that made us feel a bit calm: the Tabernacle.

For those who don't know, the Tabernacle is a box affixed to the rear of the church behind the altar where the sacred bread and wine are stored. These elements are utilized during the Holy Mass, with Catholics viewing them as the actual body and blood of Christ. In our faith, we firmly believe that it is truly the physical presence of Christ, making the Tabernacle the most sacred and significant area within any church. Only the priest is allowed to touch these once blessed and consecrated. Even then, he must pray several prayers of holiness to cleanse himself before he does so.

The tabernacle which was made purely of wood had multiple hack marks on it. It looked like axes had been used by multiple people to break into it, but while the wood outside the tabernacle was chipped beyond recognition, the box didn't break. Hence, the simple bread and wine that lay inside, remained intact and safe.

"It is a miracle, and this is what I wanted you to see, boys," Sister Mary said. "Even in all the madness, rage and hatred, Jesus could not be touched by these monsters."

Sister Mary turned to us and said, "The priest would like to meet you all now."

The parish priest walked in, and we were stunned by what we saw: his face was bruised and swollen, he had a withered look on his face that belied a broken interior, but he was full of energy. Despite having suffered at the hands of those men in the previous days, he said with a bright smile, "Good morning, children."

He welcomed us to his parish.

"I'm really sorry that you had to see it this way. But I want to show you something amazing." He turned towards the tabernacle and said, "Despite all the hate that surrounded us over the last couple of days, one thing that remains true is Jesus, who is love. Love could not be destroyed by hate as you can see right here."

I stood there entranced, unable to move, as I heard the words leave his mouth.

This was something that would stay with me for the rest of my life. A twelve-year-old Anthony surrounded by the result of violent, unhinged hatred. Yet, in front of him was the pure symbol of love. Hate simply did not win that day.

We looked around and took it all in. It was heartbreaking and devastating. It was something no human being should ever have to suffer for their faith. Yet, here we were, thousands of miles away from the Babri Masjid, in India, where a religion that had nothing to do with the violence and the atrocities that had been committed, had to suffer at the hands of another religion's fundamentalists in Pakistan.

I don't know if any of those people ever got caught, arrested, or punished. But I know this: God never forgets His own. We left the church that day with a renewed understanding of what it really meant to believe and be responsible for one's faith, and what it really meant when Jesus said, "Forgive your enemies." Sister Mary would never let us forget that moment. I will never forget it for the rest of my life.

It's ironic how a single event can alter your view of the country you consider home. I never truly sensed any distinct feelings of being a different kind of Pakistani. I always identified as Pakistani. I sang the same patriotic tunes. I recited the same National Anthem and memorized all the same verses by Allama Iqbal that all Muslim Pakistanis did. I participated in Independence Day festivities, donned national attire, and conversed in Sindhi and Punjabi.

I guess Dad's clout and sporting legend, as well as the public perception of him and our family, sheltered me from a lot of what my fellow Christians were facing across the country. Not just my fellow Christians, but Hindus, Parsis, Ahmadis and so many other minorities.

I was just twelve years old. What else would I have expected? That was the age when I was meant to enjoy the beauty of childhood as I grew older.

Overnight, because of Babri Masjid, I had become acutely aware of who I was and why all Christian children were told to be careful in Muslim communities, as regards what we said. We were told very clearly that our neighbours, family, friends, etc. were Muslims and were all great, regular people.

But we were told to be careful, to be quiet and be very observant of our surroundings. We were admonished to never get into religious discussions with anyone, even if they were our friends, and to never talk about what happened in India or the differences between Hindus and Muslims. Most importantly, we were told to not let anyone influence what we believed based on their ignorance. We were taught very clearly to practice the teachings of Jesus when He said that if somebody slapped you, you should turn the other cheek so that they could slap you on the other one. It could be very confusing for a young child in Pakistan who saw his heroes on television fighting against the villains. When a villain does something wrong to you, the hero always saves the day. So, why were we being told to be quiet?

That morning, a twelve-year-old saw a major symbol of his faith being hacked to bits with axes by an unruly mob. For some reason, we had to suffer the demolition of our church here in Pakistan. Why? Why must I pretend that everything was okay? Why did I have to be careful about what I said and to whom I said it? I had to play a good Pakistani.

I knew right there and then that there would always be an Anthony before the Babri Masjid atrocity, and an Anthony after the Babri Masjid atrocity—an Anthony whose memory of Pakistan was frozen in time to the day before 6 December, 1992, but whose life continues in a Pakistan unfamiliar to him today.

Chapter Eight

School's Out

"School is a lot like toilet paper; you only miss it when it's gone." – Anonymous

C artoons at 7:20 am.
I don't think it ever struck me how much I made Mum pull her hair out regarding reaching school in time for the 7:30am assembly.

PTV always played a three-minute cartoon at 7:20 am on school days. It wasn't my fault, was it? Thankfully, school was a three-minute walk away too, if I hurried. Mum had–much to her embarrassment–arranged for a private school bus to pick me up at 7:25am and drop me off at school before assembly began. I was always rushing to the gate before it closed, and by now, Uncle Shams, the security guard was aware that I'd be there just before the bell was rung. So, he'd hold the gate open for me, only to slam it shut the moment I sneaked in.

St Lawrence's Boys' School was probably the most known education facility in Garden East, Garden West and Soldier Bazaar. While other good schools existed in these suburbs, it was my school that was connected to the large Church and parish, as well as to the biggest college in the area: St Lawrence's Girls' College, where Sue attended.

It also helped that the principal of the boys' school was Peter D'Souza, someone whom Mum and Dad considered the best school administrator in the city. I didn't know about that, but I did know that I liked Sir Peter. He was strict but very smart, and he always started fun activities for all of us in school.

St Lawrence's was fun. We had a great football and basketball field, but it was not like the ones on TV. Ours had sand instead of grass. But that was okay because I didn't think we had enough water to maintain a grass pitch.

I was in third grade at this time, and our class teacher was Ms Alia. She was pretty and her daily outfit was a slim shalwar qameez and dupatta, like the one Sri Devi wore in Chandni. One of the boys in class, whose name is Aashiq, coincidentally, had a crush on her. One day, he even brought her a rose. We couldn't stop sniggering at our desks when Aashiq walked up to her at the start of the class to offer her the flower. She blushed and accepted it gracefully; she tugged at his cheek and said, "Thank you". Aashiq never looked as happy as he did when he walked back to his desk. The rest of us may have been laughing at him, but each of us secretly wished we had presented her with the rose instead.

Our desks were constantly being painted over. It was because every student who sat on one wrote on it with a pen or scratched their names into the wood with a protractor. We moved from the first class on the floor to the second one next to it, and the desks here were bigger. The paint this year was dark green, and it peeled off easily. So, Ms Alia told us all that if we didn't want her to become strict with us, we shouldn't peel off the paint. We agreed and peeled off the paint under the desks instead.

I didn't have to worry about spending money at recess, by the way. All the other students queued at the tuck shop, where Uncle Clifford handed over colas and samosas to everyone for between 1 and 4 rupees. That was a LOT of money. We didn't have that kind of money, so every morning just before recess began, Mum prepared breakfast and brought it to school for me to eat.

And every morning, it was one of the same two meals: piping hot porridge or French toast. Mum patiently waited at the foot of those long stairs for me to appear, and then we'd sit at the small entrance door of the church hall. It didn't matter what the weather was, or whether I was not hungry. Mum brought the breakfast, and I had to eat. I didn't regret it, because it meant I could save up my daily pocket money of 1 rupee.

I had my eye on a watch. During one of the rides home from school, Aunty Patricia had to take a detour to drop off another student; she said she'd drop me off after him. As we waited for that student's mother to come down to the roadside to collect him, I stepped out of the van for a moment as I saw a tiny little watch shop nearby. I told Aunty Patricia about it, and she said she'd wait. I ran over and looked at the twenty-or-so watches that lay in his viewing case. On the side, was a bright red digital watch that had a black border, and it looked incredible. I asked the watchmaker how much it was, and he said, "twenty-five rupees."

I had never seen twenty-five rupees in my entire life. So, I knew that I couldn't buy it then. But I made up my mind that I would save up, somehow.

From that moment on, every time I found some coins in the house, I'd keep them. I'd also save my one-rupee daily pocket money. I figured that Mum brought breakfast anyway, and I didn't 'need' the cola I had every evening when we went down to play.

It wasn't easy, however. on some days, Mum wasn't able to give me that one rupee. But that was okay, since I didn't spend a single paisa from my savings anyway. On some days, I'd ask Aunty Patricia to drive by the watch shop again so that I could make sure it was still there, and the shopkeeper would smile and tell me, "It's here, don't worry."

Finally, the big day arrived. I counted each note and coin carefully, and it was a total of twenty-five rupees. I had enough to buy my watch! Mum laughed and told me to wait and took my coins to replace them with more notes. "You'll lose the coins from your pocket as you run; carry notes instead."

The next morning, I told Aunty Patricia that I was going to buy the watch. She agreed to take me there, with a huge grin on her face. After school, she drove me there and I ran up to the shop.

However, there was no watch. It was no longer in the case and there was no other one like it. The shopkeeper was inside, and I called out to him. He saw my sad face and asked what happened. I told him I wanted to buy the watch that was there, and I had the money. He laughed and said, "Hold on a minute." I saw him come to the case, reach down under it, beyond where I could see, and pull out a small plastic wrapper which had the watch inside it.

"I knew you'd finally buy this watch someday, because you kept coming here to look at it. So, I kept it aside, otherwise someone else could have bought it. I saved it for you." I was so elated; he started grinning as if he'd bought candy for a kid. I paid him and quickly asked him to set the time. I snatched it from his hand and waved goodbye with a loud appreciation as I ran back to the van. All the kids in the van and Aunty Patricia wanted to see the watch. I slowly and deliberately put it on my wrist, enjoying the attention and feeling like a grown-up, since I had bought it with my own money after saving up. I was really proud of myself.

A Word's Worth

When I was in fourth grade, I was finally allowed to go to the school library on the first floor. Before then, I had only managed to steal a peek into it when passing by its doors, on my way to religion class. My classmates and I weren't allowed to enter because we were not the right age at the time. It was partly because the library was new.

Now, we were at the right age, and our first-ever library period was about to begin. I excitedly rushed in with the rest of my classmates and gazed in awe at the rows of bookshelves that lined the walls of the long hallway in the library. At the centre of the room was a long table with chairs all around it. A large sign screamed 'silence' at the top of every bookshelf.

I started walking around to see which books were there. Science, Mathematics, Physics, Chemistry, Biology, Social Studies—all the boring books adorned the shelves that made up that corner of the library. But as I kept walking, I saw signs that read Science Fiction, Fantasy, Adventure, Thriller, Action, Detective... Detective? I took a step back and looked at the books on this bookshelf. There were hundreds, stacked by title.

Hardy Boys, Nancy Drew, Secret Seven, Famous Five, Tom Swift... so many books to choose from.

I was yet to understand how libraries worked, so I took a book and sat down, trying to read it as fast as I could. The librarian walked over and asked why I was flipping through the pages so quickly. She laughed kindly when I told her that I was trying to finish it before the bell would be rung in forty minutes. She informed me that I could take the book home, as long as I returned it the following week. My world is shaken. I felt like someone just gave me a ticket to Disneyland. Everything changed for me from that moment.

I took the book home and read it properly this time, finishing it in two days. I returned it on the third day, hoping that I would be allowed to take another book without having to wait another week. This made me more excited, and within days, I was obsessed with the library. I read everything I could find. I even fought with my friends who wanted a book that was in the series that I was reading. Nothing would stand in my way of reading as much as I could. I was no longer a child of this world. I was a citizen of paper and thought, and my mind was a playground of the fantasies of other writers. My imagination was no longer limited to television and cartoons. For the first time in my life, I didn't fear not having friends.

I started to stay at home more, refusing to leave my room until I finished another book. I finished all 58 Hardy Boys books in one summer. I read all of the available Nancy Drew novels, of which the school had only eighty. I then finished every single Tom Swift novel as well. That was when the librarian decided that it was time for me to consider something different. She handed me a copy of The Hobbit, written by a man named Tolkien. It looked boring, with a simple brown cover, gold inscriptions, and a picture of a ring in the middle. I didn't see why this was better than Tom Swift, but she urged me to read the first chapter as a dare.

Middle Earth sucked me in, and my world became engulfed with dwarves and hobbits. The Hobbit led me to ask the librarian for other recommendations and I was pushed into the world of Ender's Game, a new book about a boy who saved the universe.

Sir Peter was told about how much I was reading lately, and he invited me to his office to talk about what I liked reading the most. I told him that it was the adventure novels that really gripped me. He led me to the library to look at a bookshelf I had previously ignored because it had 'Classic Literature' written on it, and all the books on it looked brown, beige and boring. He reached to the top of the shelf and pulled out a book titled Treasure Island, written by a man named R. L. Stevenson. "Read this, and tell me what you think about it," Sir Peter said.

I started to read it and finished the entire book in three days. I returned it to the library and then told Sir Peter how much I enjoyed it. He told me that it was part of next year's English literature class, and that I would be reading many more of such books as part of the syllabus. I couldn't believe my ears. Adventures? Part of school?

We read all the classics: Robinson Crusoe, A Tale of Two Cities, Tom Sawyer, Moby Dick, The Count of Monte Cristo, and my favourite of them all, King Solomon's Mines by H. Rider Haggard. I picked up the book only because Dad told me about it. He gave me a summary of the story, and I was riveted. I finished the book in one day, and I was thrilled to experience what its pages had in store.

The library changed my life forever. But it also turned me into a book-wormed introvert. I hardly saw my friends anymore because I was always in my room, reading something new. Mum bought me a set of the Tell Me Why series and we subscribed to the Reader's Digest monthly novels. Life and all its excitement now stay only in my imagination.

Prelude to a Kite Runner

The annual elocution competition had been announced, and Mum wanted me to register for it. I was in fifth grade and hated speaking in public. Still, I noticed that Rodney and his elder brother, Sheldon, registered for it. So, I figured that it'd be fun. Sheldon, who was one grade higher than Rodney and I, decided to recite O Captain, My Captain! by Walt Whitman, which we hadn't studied in our grade yet. I remember the poem because Dad recited it to me whenever he was in the mood to flex his literary muscles.

I realised that there was no way I could compete with Sheldon's recitation, as he was the best elocutioner in the school. His style of expression and his command of the language were second to none, while I still struggled with apostrophes and the spelling of 'heir'. I thought the rule was to put i before e except after c.

Our English teacher gave me a poem she thought that I could recite well. It was a short, three-stanza piece on the life of a kite and its journey from being held in the hands of a child to being thrown in the air, only to be whisked away by the wind. It seemed easy enough, and I didn't have any desire to turn this into a competition. So, I agreed.

On the morning of the recital, all the students gathered in the church hall, where a stage had been set up. The teacher came up to me before I left the class, handing me a paper kite she'd bought the night before. It was a simple, but beautiful piece. It was beige in colour and was shaped like a long-tailed diamond, like the kites we saw in paintings. She told me to make sure I threw this kite into the air once I reached the stanza about the wind.

I was caught by a sudden stage fright, as I wondered how ridiculous it would look. Here I was, surrounded by boys who recited Wordsworth, Whitman and Marlowe, while I'd be talking about a kite and throwing stuff in the air. Somehow, she convinced me to calm down.

I proceed to the hall. Rodney took to the stage, to perform, and Sheldon's recital elicited the loudest applause from all and sundry. My name was finally called, and I nervously ambled onto the stage, trying to find the middle. I almost fell off when I came too close to the edge. Nervous coughs from the faculty echoed and my classmates sniggered among themselves. No one noticed the kite I was holding because I had hidden it behind my back and laid it down at the edge of the stage when no one had been paying attention.

I launched into my recital, flailing my arms around dramatically, for effect, because I knew the poem itself was simple.

As I neared the stanza with the wind reference, I moved towards the edge of the stage and picked up the kite. Upon reciting the verse, I flung the kite into the air at an angle, not really paying attention to how it should be done. As luck would have it, the kite sliced through the air in a way that allowed it to fly high towards the roof, and then glide gracefully across the long hallway, to the other end, landing directly in front of the judges.

The audience of students gasped and laughed at the apparent audacity, reacting further with rapturous applause, while the teachers all had grins on their faces at the ridiculousness of it all. I finished the poem and went off the stage. After an hour of other recitals, the judges deliberated over the winners and announced the top three prizes for various categories.

Surprisingly, my name was called as the winner of the primary elocution stage. No one was more surprised than I was, or so I thought. Sheldon looked more surprised than I did, because they declared him as the second-place winner, all because I threw a kite into the air.

I loved school.

Brass Balls

The following summer, Peter D'souza, our Principal, made an announcement during assembly that he was initiating the first-ever school band for St Lawrence's. He said something about him wanting to make us as formidable as the celebrated brass band of St Patrick's School in Saddar, renowned for its accomplishments and its consistent wins in the inter-school band competition of Karachi.

He invited boys in all grades to join, and to meet him in the school hall at 10am during recess. I immediately signed up, and so did most of my friends. We didn't know what a school band did, but he had mentioned something about musical instruments, and we wanted to be a part of it simply because we wanted to be seen as musicians.

During recess, we gathered in the assembly area where we saw him being joined by a short, older gentleman who walked with a formidable, steady gait and deliberate footsteps. "This..." Sir Peter announced, "is our new bandmaster." He formerly trained and ran the brass band for the Pakistan Armed Forces in Karachi. His job, we were told, was to whip us into a class act, and not just in terms of musical performance, but also in marching.

We were given the choice of a variety of instruments—flutes, recorders, trumpets, trombones, tubas, snare drums, tenor drums, bass drums, cymbals, timpani and more. I chose the flute because I thought it was cool. It was also because I tried to pick up the drums, but my rhythm was so horrible that the bandmaster didn't know whether to laugh or get angry.

Thus began months of double weekly practices. Each session pushed us to our limits as we delved into learning chords, notes, reading music sheets, and mastering the use of our breath, lungs, diaphragms, and fingers. Some of us even mastered circular breathing to ensure we never missed a note due to running out of breath.

The songs we learned were a plethora of classic Pakistani and subcontinental melodies, including the national anthem, Iqbal's poems put to music, Punjabi folk music, like Latthe di chadar, and more.

The most challenging part was still ahead of us, because after we became proficient with the instruments, we were required to march while playing. We experienced everything from getting a light whip on our shins for not marching in sync, to being forced to kneel on the side of the field for repeatedly missing the same steps. In time, however, the bandmaster succeeded, and so did we.

We celebrated the School Festival on August 10, which was also the feast day of St Lawrence and the Church. Guests from the parish families, students' families, and the bishop's office were invited to join us for the event. During the festival, we showcased a performance of the school song, and I made sure to memorise every word and tune to make it a memorable day.

"We are students of dear St Lawrence's School
And we're happy to be so
For united we stand, and divided fall
All through the years we go
Oh, St Lawrence's School we shall love thee
With a love that will never end"

The audience and guests were left in awe as we executed a march and seamlessly positioned ourselves to spell out the school's initials, SLBS. The thunderous applause and standing ovation from the crowd filled us with immense joy and pride.

I hadn't felt a thrill like this in my life, and it was only a fraction of the pride that I was going to feel soon.

After the feast day, Sir Peter gathered us once again in the assembly area to inform us that St Lawrence's Boys School would compete in the inter-school band competition, taking on the famed school bands of St Patrick's, St Joseph's and St Paul's. We were meant to put our heart and soul into practice for this event, taking place just one month from that day.

The day arrived, and we started off early in the morning at 6:30am to reach the venue in Clifton, near Jahangir Kothari Parade. A sea of crisp and bright white uniforms alighted from the school buses hired for us, with our maroon ties smartly contrasting against our uniforms. I polished my silver flute to a bright sheen and practised all night at home.

The event kicked off, as St Patrick's stole the show with an impressive spectacle that could easily grace the television screen. Their extraordinary brass band boasted an array of instruments, some of which I had never even laid eyes on before.

Afterwards, it was our moment to shine as we stepped into the spotlight. Our performance took centre stage, featuring the renowned Pakistan Armed Forces song 'Allah O Akbar,' which had gained recent popularity on radio and TV. We followed it up with our national anthem, and to conclude, we showcased our incredible marching skill while performing synchronised movements and spelling letters out for the judges using our bodies' positions.

Our performance netted us second place, which was a surprise to all since this was our debut performance. Our school had never had a band before, and to win the penultimate prize of the city's band contests meant the world to us.

To celebrate, Sir Peter took the entire band to Funland, the theme park in Clifton that I always loved going to. Unfortunately, Mum could only take I and Sue there whenever Dad sent us money.

When we got there, we had one more surprise. Sir Peter arranged for halwa puri as a celebratory breakfast for everyone. He was a sweet man.

Surprise, Astaghfirullah!

The influence of my classmates and the mosque near my home, as well as my closest friends Bubloo and Sadiq had a tremendous impact on the things I learned about the Muslim culture. PTV aired a lot of Islamic programmes and Quranic recitations, further strengthening this impact.

When I got into the seventh grade, I had memorized nearly all of the significant Muslim prayers. The Hamd, a prayer dedicated to praising Allah, and the Naat, a prayer honouring Muhammad, the Islamic prophet, were required components in our school's Urdu textbooks that every student, regardless of their religion, had to commit to memory. The Sindh Textbook Board made it compulsory, as part of the primary school curriculum, even requiring Catholic students in our Catholic school to learn and recite them in order to pass our routine Urdu exams.

I didn't know it, but Dad told me that this was a form of indoctrination by the Sindh government.

"Why on earth is a non-Muslim child made to learn Islamic prayers in order to pass out of school, for a language subject?" he would ask his friends whenever they came over for tea. It must be done, they'd tell him.

Dad turned to me and told me to learn it for the exam and forget about it once I was done. He thought it was not fair to force a Christian to learn Muslim prayers just to pass out of school.

"John, it's happening everywhere; they'll have to do this every year. You know that," Uncle Raju told Dad. Uncle Raju was Dad's best friend, and a professor at the DJ Sindh Government Science College. Uncle Raju attended St Andrews Church in Saddar, and along with Dad, was very upset at the way things had been going on in Pakistan for Christians, particularly the Urdu-speaking believers who faced the worst brunt of anti-minority violence.

"They'll make our people do sanitary work in the sewers and sweep the streets just because we're Christians. You think they're going to stop making our kids learn Muslim prayers?" Uncle Raju said to Dad.

Dad sighed and said, "Forget it, yaar; there's no point. I had to deal with this nonsense when I was in my prime. My God was more important to the selectors than my legs in the 70s. Now, my children have to deal with it too. I'll get them out of Pakistan the first chance I get."

I was getting uncomfortable with the conversation because I didn't understand what was happening. I thought Dad was famous in Pakistan and everyone loved him; it seemed I might have been wrong.

What made things different for me, however, was that I absorbed information like a sponge at this point. By listening to prayers being broadcast on television, I learned the Kalima, Ayat-ul-Kursi, and each of the five different prayers for the various parts of the day, including Fajr, Zuhr, Asr, Maghrib and Isha prayers. I even knew some of the Friday 'Juma'ah' prayers. Because I loved Urdu and Arabic calligraphy after discovering this art in Saudi Arabia, I also knew how to write the prayers in Arabic with all their intonations and accents.

All of these resulted in hilarious, and somewhat embarrassing, incidents for my Muslim classmates at school.

One day, the school board decided to send its school inspectors to monitor the quality of the facilities and teaching methodology. All the students were told to be on their best behaviour. We were to ensure that our uniforms were neatly pressed and pristine white, our shoes polished to a shiny black, our hair was to be cut short, and of course, the teachers were to be on their best behaviour too. They were not permitted to at us that morning, unlike most other days.

One of the inspectors decided to come into my class during the Urdu lessons. He was clearly a Muslim with a long beard, a shaven upper lip and a prayer cap. He was quite courteous and respectful, proceeding to observe the lesson being taught.

Suddenly, he interrupted the teacher to ask if anyone could recite the Hamd. I quickly raised my hand first, and the teacher was perplexed. She wasn't sure whether to allow me to recite it since I was Catholic. The inspector already saw me. He asked for my name, and I proclaimed it quite loudly. Hearing the name, 'Anthony' surprised him. He asked if I was sure I wanted to recite Hamd. I said 'yes' and went ahead to recite it fluently. I had only finished two stanzas before he raised his hand to silence me.

"Very good; well done," he remarked. The teacher seized this moment to puff her chest out and tell him "he's a Christian boy and still knows our prayers so well." This made me smirk since I wasn't sure if my boldness went down well with her. A few minutes later, the inspector asked if anyone could recite the Naat. Again, I raised my hand in the air, above my head, eagerly hoping that he'd choose me again. This time, however, he said loudly, "Anyone else?" The teacher smirked a bit differently.

Later, after class, I heard some of the students talking. One of them pointed to me and said, "Saala choora harami." I had never heard this term before, so I asked Mum about it later. She got angry with me, wondering why I wanted to use such a term. "It's an insult, Anthony. They use that term to refer to us because they believe that we are only fit to clean sewers. Who said this to you? I want to know." I was too afraid to tell her. I didn't want the boys in school to come after me for snitching on them. The next day, my mum complained to the principal.

Outshining Muslim students at their own religion wasn't something we are meant to do in this country, it seems, as I would learn in the coming years.

Chura and Bhangi (an untouchable caste in India, whose members are mostly assigned sweeping and cleaning jobs that no one else wants to do), were two words I kept hearing in school from that day. Sometimes, students said it to my face; sometimes, behind my back. The way they laughed suggested that they didn't know what it meant, but that someone told them to say it. Or maybe they saw someone saying it to someone else. Mum said that they learned the words at home.

I hated those words. I didn't like the feeling I got when I heard them.

The Life of Sigh

If there's one thing I didn't expect to learn in the eighth grade, it was how to perfect the art of irritating our teachers. A friend of mine in my class, Jibran, excelled in this art and decided to introduce us to it. He dared one of us to be his first prank starter. Ghazanfar decided to volunteer.

The first lesson? The after effect.

He gave Ghazanfar the samosa he'd bought from the canteen during recess that day.

"Just before Sir Nicholas comes into the classroom, after this teacher leaves, run to the teacher's seat and rub the samosa crust all over the seat. But make sure the oil isn't obvious."

We stared in awe at Jibran. This would leave a very obvious stain–possibly difficult to remove—on the seat, and consequently, Sir Nicholas' trousers. It was gloriously diabolical.

Ghazanfar was terrified. "It'll ruin his trousers! He'll find out it can't be removed when he gets home and the Principal will come after me!"

But Jibran had planned it out perfectly. "No, he won't. This is the last class of the day. After this, we all go home, so he won't go into the faculty room. Hence, no teacher would notice and tell him. He'll go out to the parking lot and students will laugh at him when they see it. He'll only realise it when he gets home, and by that time, it could have been caused by anything. He'll never be able to blame the students."

It was genius... and it worked. Ghazanfar did the prank, and since some of us were friends with Carl, Sir Nicholas' son, we heard about this later when we found out he was trying to figure out where he stained his trousers.

On another occasion, we superglued the blackboard duster to the teacher's table. Everyone was made to march to the assembly and kneel in front of the whole school, the next morning.

It was worth it.

Perhaps, the greatest prank of all–and also one we regretted instantly–was the one we played on Miss Rubina, one of the school's loveliest teachers. For some reason, we thought that it'd be fun and that she would react positively. Unfortunately, the prank we had in mind didn't go quite well, and it ended up with her qameez being stained at the front with ink. It was still only 11am, which meant that she had to walk around school with that. I believe she had a bad morning, as she seemed less jovial compared to the time before we pranked her. It reduced her to tears, and she started crying in the classroom, looking at us with disappointed eyes, as she ran out of the classroom.

We were floored. The fun of the prank instantly got replaced by the wall of shame that our hearts crashed into. The class became so quiet that you could hear the sound of a pin dropping. None of us dared to look at one another, lest we recognised the indignity we felt, reflected on another person's face.

We felt terrible about what we had done, but suddenly, like a slow wave at the beach, another feeling started to overcome the shame.

Fear.

She had obviously gone to the principal to complain, and he was the scariest principal we had ever had. What made it worse wasn't that it was Sir Michael who'd reprimand us, but that he'd bring Sir Abdon as well.

Sir Abdon was a giant man, who stood at 6'5" and towered over everyone in the school. He usually visited the gym, and he was also muscular. He was also the administrator whose responsibility was to punish us at the assembly ground if we hadn't cut our nails, polished our shoes or cut our hair. The punishments were brutal, but the one I hated most was when he placed a pencil between our fingers and crushed our hands in his, making the pain sear through our arm. While many of us had grown accustomed to it and didn't cry anymore, the ones who faced it for the first time learned immediately to never cross Sir Abdon.

Sure enough, within minutes, both sirs were in the classroom. Their faces were deadpan as they asked us a simple question: who masterminded it? None of us uttered a word. So, they decided to punish the entire class.

We didn't know where Miss Rubina went, but we collectively, silently vowed amongst ourselves to never prank another teacher again.

The next day, many of us brought flowers, sweets, cards and other gifts for her and inundated her with apologies. She forgave us all, but not before giving us a much-needed lecture.

It's funny how school teaches you more than just sin, cos and tan.

Perfect Prefect

When I got into the ninth grade, Sir Michael, our new principal, and a formidable man who reminded me of Muhammad Ali, the American boxer, called me to his office. He was seated with my class teacher. They both invited me to try to convince me to accept the position of a class prefect. This was the position that students get, which gives them additional responsibilities of monitoring, not just their classes, but other classes on the same floor. It was fun, because it gave one the opportunity to intimidate the younger kids, and wander around the school during certain classes, when one's name was on the roster. The main goal, however, is to catch truants in the act, or students who've disappeared to a corner of the school to play around while having told their teacher they're going to the toilets.

I was happy to accept, and I realised that my best friend, Sadiq Saleem, was also going to be a monitor. We were in the same class, and we spent practically every minute of the day together, usually at his place, after school.

We also got cool, dark, blue gowns to wear over our uniforms, which we all agreed was the best reason.

A year of shenanigans followed. Sadiq and I joined other prefects to have fun at the expense of the other students, particularly the youngest ones who thought they were amazing. We convinced some of the kids near the canteen to share their lunch with us, telling them that they'd be in our good books. A year of free samosas, chocolates and Pepsi followed. I knew that I was going to hell for this at some point, but when you're thirteen, none of this really matters to you.

I still had to focus on making sure I hit the right grades for class, according to Dad. While Mum was over the moon with me being a prefect, Dad was still concerned I'd let it get to my head. Rightly so, during mock exams before the ninth-grade boards, I failed the Sindhi language one. Sindhi, being the provincial language, was hard enough as it was, and my lack of attention didn't make it any better to learn.

Mum got furious because she didn't want Dad to know that I had thrown away almost eight years of A-grade results across all subjects, just because I now had a gown on my shoulders.

She signed me up for Sindhi tuition with a family that lived behind Faria Apartments. The girl who taught me was a beautiful woman who looked like a cross between Audrey Hepburn and Sri Devi. So, I paid attention and made sure I didn't annoy her in any way. I studied with her every day for two months, and she was convinced that I was going to pass.

Then the Boards began.

To everyone's surprise–mostly mine—I didn't just pass the Sindhi board exam, I got the highest marks and a distinction. The months of work we put in paid off and I became the talk of the school. The Catholic, English-speaking Tamil boy who outperformed the ethnic native students in his school. Nay! In his city.

Head in the Clouds

The moment I got into grade ten, the final and senior-most grade in Pakistan's matriculation system (high school starts from grade 11), I got called once again by Sir Michael to his office. This time, I knew what it was about.

Rumours had already started to spread in the school about which students would get nominated to be Head Prefect–the person to whom all prefects and monitors report, and who reports directly to the principal. Among the candidates were I and Sadiq. I was convinced Sadiq would get picked, but there were things I hadn't considered. Mum was on the Catholic School Board in Karachi, and there hadn't been a Catholic Head Prefect in this Catholic school in years. Rumours abound that I'd be picked simply because of those two reasons.

The rumours came true, but that didn't make me happy, however. Surely, I got to wear the much-coveted maroon gown over my shoulders and had a special badge as well. Yet, I had never led any team before, and I did not have the presence or personality of someone who needed to be strict, formidable and tough.

I was jovial, full of fun, non-confrontational. How was I going to manage prefects who were bigger than I was, and students who were part of cliques that were known to cause trouble in school?

It turned out that these things didn't matter. By simply having Mum involved in the board, I managed to get away with quite a lot. I say quite a lot and not everything because even fate and influence couldn't protect me from my own folly. At least once a month I would arrive late for assembly and would be made to kneel down at the back of the rows of students, easily seen from the classrooms with my gown flowing in the wind. Why? Because I wanted to stay at home and watch early morning cartoons on PTV.

One specific time I was called to Sir Michael's office again. This time, I was given a dressing down because I had a lapse in thinking and took a pair of knuckle dusters to show off to my friends in class, but the teacher caught me.

I didn't learn my lesson, obviously, because just a few months later, I brought to school a gift that I had received during my holidays in Saudi Arabia. It was a small 6-inch retractable pocketknife–the sort you see in muggings on TV. I found the knife to be something to brag about to friends… nothing more.

However, what I didn't know was that possessing any pocketknife that was 6 inches or above was considered dangerous enough to be a criminal offence. This was a fact that Sir Michael didn't allow me to forget, as another student snitched, and my schoolbag got searched. In both situations, Sir Michael ensured to remind me of how I had a legacy to uphold, and how my family name depended on me.

I hated that people did this, but I understand their point now that I've grown older. When I was in fifth grade, I used to be annoyed even if I took pride in Dad's name. Five years later, I had become cognisant of how a name can impact an entire generation. This is especially true when you're a minority in a country where people are obsessed with finding faults in not just you or your family, but in your religion and ethnicity too.

Chapter Nine

The Festival

"Anthony, Ingeva!"

Mum yelled out in Tamil from the bedroom. Ingeva was one of only two Tamil words I know, meaning 'come here'.

The other was 'dostron', which means 'welcome' in Tamil. Usually, you'd say it while holding your palms together like the Hindus do when they say 'Namaste'. Amma taught me these two words when I was seven. Now, I was thirteen, but I didn't know any other word because Mum never taught me. She was learning English and Urdu and didn't want to confuse Sue and me. She wanted us to excel in English so that we could go to good universities one day.

I ran to her, and she had just finished ironing the orange vest that I was to wear.

It was the first day of the 'Our Lady of Vailankanni' festival–my favourite festival of the year, after Christmas. I knew that my friends would be coming too, so I was excited. Well, not just any friends, but the friend I had a crush on. We were always friends, but a few months before, we met at a wedding, and we reconnected strongly. I think it was because of the song Candi Periera from the band Milestones was singing. We decided to dance to it on the dance floor and ended up dancing with each other all night long.

Mum grabbed me and told me to try it on, because she wasn't sure if it'd still fit me. It did, so she went to get Sue's orange kurta ready.

It was September, and I remember Sister Mary telling us the reason the festival took place in September was that it was the month of Mary. I loved Mother Mary. I thought that she was so beautiful, but also because she took care of Baby Jesus. She's the reason we had Christmas. I also felt a bit wary of her because her festival time meant lots of rosaries, and I got easily bored during rosaries. We kept saying the same thing over and over again. Why couldn't we try something new? It was always Joyful, Sorrowful and Glorious mysteries. Weren't there more? Plus, how did adults keep track of how many Hail Marys they recited? I kept forgetting, even though I had a rosary in my hands. I skipped beads because I kept daydreaming. If I was saying a decade, I would look at Mum to tell me that I'd finished ten Hail Marys, otherwise, Mother Mary would be upset with me.

Sister Mary told me the story of the festival this year, since we were finally old enough to understand it. 'She's called Our Lady of Good Health', and appeared to people in Vailankanni, Tamil Nadu, in India. I didn't know that! Vailankanni is close to where my family is from, which is what Dad had told me.

The tale was from the 16th century, during the time the Portuguese were in Goa. At the time, a young Tamil boy was carrying buttermilk to give to a man who lived a distance away from his home. At one point, the boy wanted to rest his feet from the hot sun, so he stopped near a lake, under the shade of a Banyan tree.

Suddenly, a beautiful woman who was carrying an infant in her arms appeared to him, bathed in light. She asked the boy for milk to feed her baby. The boy was so entranced with her beauty and quiet demeanour that he gave her the milk immediately. She fed her child and thanked him.

He felt energised from the encounter and ran with the milk to deliver it to the man. He apologized for the delay, as well as the fact that there was less milk in the pot. However, when the man opened the cover, he found that the milk was almost overflowing. The boy went home confused.

It didn't end there. Another boy encountered the lady. He was disabled and lame in one leg. He too was selling milk, and he found a spot near the Banyan tree, preferring to sell it to passersby. Unfortunately, he rarely received customers. One day, a woman appeared to him holding a baby. The boy was concerned about having enough to sell, but he still gave her a cup of buttermilk, which she used to feed her baby.

When she was done feeding her baby, she asked the boy to go to Nagapattinam and look for a Catholic man there. "Tell him to build a chapel at Vailankanni in my honour." The boy, suddenly full of energy, ran to Nagapattinam without realising he was no longer limping. He found the man and shared the story. The man remembered the earlier story of a young boy, and now faced with a similar tale, he believed that the woman was Mother Mary. He got together with the Catholic men of Nagapattinam to build a chapel at Vailankanni as she requested, and the Church dedicated it to the Blessed Virgin Mary, calling her "Our Lady of Good Health," after seeing the healing of the boy's leg.

Sister Mary explained that in the 17th century, a Portuguese merchant ship sailing from Macau to Ceylon (Sri Lanka today) got caught in a storm at sea, in the Bay of Bengal, south of India. Being Portuguese, the sailors prayed fervently all night for Mother Mary, who was called Star of the Sea, to pray for their salvation from the storm.

They promised to build a church in her honour in the place they would find land if they survived. The story goes that the sea became still as if the storm had never taken place, and they saw land in the distance. Sailing towards it, they dropped anchor and asked what the place was called.

It was Vailankanni, and the date they made landfall was September 8, the day of Mother Mary's birth, the Feast of the Nativity. They kept their promise and converted the existing chapel which was made of thatch into a proper stone church.

That made sense, I thought to myself, because the church where the festival happened in Karachi was St Anthony's Parish, which was an exact replica of the church in Vailankanni. I also understood why so many Tamil Catholics came there.

We started to get ready for the first day of the Novena. The Novena takes place for 9 days and ends on September 8 when we all celebrate the Feast. I love going there because it's a sea of thousands of us wearing orange, and the aroma of freshly lit incense fills the air in the neighbourhood.

It isn't just the smell of incense that I love. The aroma of freshly made sewo-boond–the little sweet balls of green, red and yellow–was my favourite thing about the festival. They distribute it to everyone in little bags after the prayers are over.

As we entered the church compound from the gate, jostling through the mighty crowd of Tamil aunties and their sarees, I looked around, trying to find my friends. All over the compound and inside the church building, all I saw was a sea of sarees, kurtas and lungis. It was the first day, and no one wanted to miss this. I had never seen such a big crowd though. It seemed like this day was special. I overheard Mum telling Amma, the other day, that a new statue of 'Our Lady of Health' had come to the church from Vailankanni and had been blessed and consecrated to St Anthony's. I didn't know what consecrated meant.

When I felt we were going to get crushed by the crowd, Mum yelled, "Over here" and pulled Sue and me to a small opening where Choti Mami was standing. Choti Mami was Amma's sister-in-law, married to Amma's brother, Kodan Mamu. I liked Choti Mami; she was always nice to me. Her daughter, Melba, was my favourite cousin, but I didn't understand why they named her after ice cream. Melba was the one who introduced me to Sri Devi, my favourite actress.

I really liked Sri Devi. I liked her so much that I had the biggest collection of postcards that had her photos. All my friends also bought me her postcards, which I put into my diary. I think I had over 400 of them, and they didn't include the magazines that had her on the cover. Filmfare, Cineblitz, Stardust... I had them all. I also had a large poster of her posing on the set of her film, Chaalbaaz.

Mum and Dad laughed at the idea of me crushing on Sri Devi, but I didn't mind. Every time her new film was released, I ran down to Feroz Bhai's shop to check if they had it for rent. One day, I learned that a film called Roop Ki Rani Choron Ka Raja was released, and it starred Sri Devi and Anil.

I also loved Anil Kapoor because of his sense of humour. His movie, Mr India, was my favourite movie of all time. I wished that I could be invisible too. But I read in Cineblitz that the new movie was their best one yet, so I asked Mum if I could stay over at Melba's home to watch it with my cousins.

I was brought back to reality when I heard the priest start with a loud "In the name of the Father..." over the mic. But he said it in Tamil, so I only knew it was time to start because Mum pinched me. Everyone started to recite the Novena and Rosary in Tamil, and I didn't understand a word. All I knew was that if he said, "Gey modavey," it meant he'd said the Hail Mary, so I recited the responding Holy Mary every time.

I always knew the Novena had ended when they sang Thaiye Kanniye, the main Marian Tamil hymn of the festival. It means My Dearest Virgin Mary in English.

This is the moment I always looked forward to. It was a weird ceremony, because all of a sudden, a long nylon rope appeared at the front of the church crowd. The rope was taken over the crowd's heads, just in reach, and everyone reached up to touch it or pull it down to kiss it. Mum told me that since not everyone can go up to the statue, the rope itself touches the statue at one end as the crowd kiss it, hoping their veneration reaches Our Lady.

Mum carried Sue, while Nyena carried me, and we kissed the rope, too. I only managed to grab it with my hands because it went over my head too fast, so I kissed my hand instead. I saw others kiss their hands after they touched the statue of Jesus or Mary, so I assumed it was okay to do this too.

Now that everything was over, it was time to leave, and Mum said that we were going to Choti Mami's home for tea. Choti Mami lived in the Plaza suburb, where the famous Jubilee Market stood. Named after the Jubilee Mansion, the name was also passed on to various other properties and the little community park in the area.

Choti Mami's home was right above a street that had a tea shop at the end. So, the whole street smelled of milky tea being brewed all day. It was probably why everyone associated her home with afternoon tea visits.

Her home was a true Karachi nuclear family testament–two rooms, shared by two families. Choti Mami and her husband, Kodan Mamu, took up one room with their six kids, Ernestine (who we called Guddi), Melba, Diana, Valerie, Gordon and Melwyn. Barri Mami, with her husband, John Paul, and their four kids, Sandra, Alice, Marilyn, Michelle and Aaron took up the other.

There was a small kitchen, a small bathroom and a small veranda. Yet, it felt like a mansion of love every time we visited. In many ways, this was the reality of many migrant Tamil families in Karachi, where everyone chose to stay either next door to or with each other, to keep the community, culture, language and history alive.

Everyone we knew in Plaza were related to Mum and Dad in some way, but mostly to Mum. Choti and Barri Mami were both married to Amma's brothers, making them my grandaunts and granduncles. But just down the road, two blocks away, lived Georgina Aunty, who was married to Uncle Anthony, Amma's eldest brother. Amma's elder sister was lovingly called Akka by everyone. Akka meant 'elder sister' in Tamil. I didn't know that and always assumed it was her name. I didn't realise how big Amma's family was until I started visiting Plaza. Across the street from both families lived Amma's other elder brother, Plaza and Jubilee were the strongholds of Karachi's Christian Tamil population, who migrated from Tamil Nadu over a century ago. Hailing from the cities of Pondicherry, Madras and mostly Vailankanni, they were numbered in thousands, including my family, as Mum and Dad told me. Initially moving to be caretakers of the Tamil-focused churches in the area and its surroundings, some also moved for the varying skilled worker opportunities including carpentry, plumbing and building works in the newly developing city. Today, the area is congested with little streets and alleys in between large century-old buildings housing families who trace their genealogy up to two hundred years in the past.

This wasn't the only Tamil stronghold, though, as Amma informed me one day. In Karachi's Madrasi Para, near the Jinnah Post-Graduate Medical Centre, lay the Tamil Hindu community of Pakistanis who migrated from Madras to come and build a new life in this city that was being developed by the British Empire. Just like the Catholics of Karachi, the Hindus here built their communities around their main temple, the Maripata Temple.

The reason Amma wanted me to know this was because of Dad. Dad's family had Hindu and Catholic roots, and some of his family stayed in Madrasi Para while most lived in the Swaminarayan Mandir community of Bolton Market. Swaminarayan Mandir recently crossed two hundred years in Pakistan, Dad told me.

Maripata Temple itself was the biggest temple Hindu temple in Karachi until this year. Just like the mobs destroyed Sacred Heart Church in Keamari, they also went after the more obvious Hindu community, because of the Ayodhya situation, and wreaked havoc at the temple, leaving terrified Hindus there with only the nearby missionary hospital in which to hide their women and children from the raging crowd who were baying for their blood.

I'm thankful that my family is safe in Plaza. Who knows how things could have gone for them too?

Now that I was a teenager, I was starting to notice things differently. I never used to understand why there was so much hate and anger among Muslims against us, Christians, in Pakistan, but now I'm getting the gist of it.

I recently went to Rainbow Centre in Saddar because I wanted Vital Signs' new album 'Hum Tum', and while I was at a shop, I saw posters across their walls and in other shops too, of Muslim preachers with really hateful words in Urdu for Christians, Jews and Hindus. It seemed like they were really angry on the poster and their audio recordings were being played in many of the shops. I'll never understand why these preachers all scream in their sermons. Why can't they speak nicely and calmly like priests do during the Mass? They have microphones, so everyone can hear them, isn't it?

I quickly bought the album and walked back to the bus stop.

This wasn't the Karachi I grew up in. I thought when I became a teenager, I'd do more things with my friends. Unfortunately, a few of my Muslim friends in Faria Apartments had started to keep a distance from me. Not Bubloo though. Bubloo and I were friends for life.

One of them even told me to my face that it was only because he knew me personally that he remained friends with me. Otherwise, he didn't like speaking to Christians because they were 'kaafir', or non-believers and that they were not to be trusted. He also hated Ahmadis a lot, which surprised me because, until that evening, he was a friendly and kind man. I didn't know what changed in just a few months. He wasn't like this earlier; he'd even helped us to build the Christmas star for two full years.

I think the worst change I noticed was fear. When I heard Dad's stories, I felt anger and helplessness exuding from them. However, I think that anger and helplessness were replaced by a sense of apprehension and concern. We were scared.

Christians in Pakistan had always been 'People of the Book' for Muslims. We shared a mutual religious history and legacy. We believed in all the same prophets with the exception of one. We believed in the Abrahamic God. Somehow, we went from People of the Book to 'people to be booked' in prison.

Dad spoke to me at length, telling me to control my tongue. "Be careful who you make friends with, beta, and make sure they're mostly Christian. You can't trust anyone in Pakistan anymore. They ratified the blasphemy laws this year, and one wrong word can send you to jail, or worse" he said.

I had never heard of blasphemy before. I asked him what it was, and he explained it. I got even more confused. Why would anyone say anything bad about their prophet in Pakistan? It made no sense. "It doesn't need to make sense, Anthony," Dad continued, with some irritation. "It just needs to fit their narrative. If they don't like you, or if they want your house, your business, your land or just simply don't want you in their neighbourhood, they can claim you blasphemed. They can't prove it, and they don't need to. It's our word against theirs."

Dad got more upset and decided to leave the conversation there. He told me to go help Mum on the balcony, as she was washing clothes.

I got up to go out of the living room, but not before wondering if this would stay this way forever.

Would we no longer make Christmas stars?

Would we no longer have the Vailankanni novena at St Anthony's?

Would we no longer enjoy Hot Cross Buns at Misquita Bakery?

I was only fourteen. I shouldn't have had to ask these questions.

Epilogue

It has been three decades since that last memory. In that time, tens of thousands of Christians have left Pakistan, migrating to Canada, Australia, the US, with some even settling in the Middle East. In this time, our fear has only grown.

Asia Bibi is an example of the system being helpless against bigotry. Even the appeals of Pope Benedict and Pope Francis to the government fell on deaf ears. Her release was only a temporary balm, as thousands of Christians still languish in prison on charges of blasphemy that mostly have no evidence, save the word of a Muslim. In many cases, the charges can't be proven as even to utter the alleged blasphemous statement is blasphemous to Muslims, hence only the implied act is taken as gospel by the Courts.

Pakola Masjid has grown even more. From its humble beginnings as a one-storey mosque it is now a two-storey mosque and madrassah, with multiple loudspeakers everywhere you looked. The muezzin who calls the azaan five times a day still has the same beautiful, seraphic voice I remember from childhood, which made the loudness seem easier to bear. When the other muezzins call out, however, it isn't really that endearing. Thousands of children learn how to read the Quran, with many become Hifz-e-Quran or someone who knows the entire book by rote. It's only during Juma'ah prayers that we find it difficult having such a popular mosque next to our home, as the parking situation on our narrow street becomes impossible to cross through.

The riots in Gojra, Punjab, in 2009 where Muslims attacked the Christian township saw eight people dead, including one child.

The Christian village of Joseph Colony was burned to the ground, displacing countless Christian families because of an accusation of blasphemy against a Christian man. Fire was set to one hundred and sixty houses, together with eighteen shops and two churches.

St Lawrence's Church, once one of the most beautiful and open parishes in Karachi, now needs armed patrols and police forces outside its gates during major festivals like Easter Sunday and Christmas. The threat of militant Islamic attacks by extremists is very real and we cannot take the risk. Muslim friends tell us that it's not that bad, but that's what they said in the days before the Easter Sunday attack in Lahore killed dozens of children and sent hundreds to hospitals. The police aren't just outside our parish; they're outside St Patrick's–that bastion of Catholic history in Pakistan. They're outside most churches at these times of the year.

Dad passed away in 2019, due to pancreatic cancer. The way the government of Pakistan treated a former Olympian and pride of the nation will never be forgotten by my family. Through a few good friends, word went up the grapevine and reached some powers that be in the state apparatus. A few days before he passed away, I received a call from the then-president of Pakistan. He enquired a bit about Dad's history, which surprised me. Wouldn't somebody have apprised him? I told him about Dad's rich legacy, his countless wins in Commonwealth and Asian games, and his days of bringing glory to the country and the flag.

The President asked me to send him Dad's CV and that "he'll see if he can do something".

That would be the last I ever heard from the government of Pakistan. The body that had been formed for life and celebrated by the nation had run its last race. And like Dad, this can be said for Christianity in the country, too. We're now holding on to our last breaths before we're forced to die out quietly.

The flag's white stripe, once symbolising minorities at Muhammad Ali Jinnah's insistence, is now only symbolic of the colour of the shroud our faiths are being wrapped in before we're all buried soon.

And yet, somehow, like that pesky plant in the beloved animated film Wall-E, hope finds a way.

The new generation of Pakistanis is fighting back. Liberal and conservative alike are pushing through the mire of Pakistan's legacy of religious fascism and are bridging toward something. We don't know what that something is, but it is clearly worth fighting for.

Adrian has built a successful career over 15 years, first working for Coke Studio with Rohail Hyatt and then remotely for an American cryptocurrency news wire. He has 2 children and a loving wife Zo. Sue and her husband Chris have two teenage kids who she insisted should be raised in Karachi after they turned 10, hoping they would learn the street smarts that helped her and me take on the world outside Pakistan.

Mum stays in her cosy little home on a lower floor in a complex near Soldier Bazaar number two, unable to climb up the flights of stairs of our four-storey family home.

Faria Apartment has changed. It is no longer the Christian-only building I remember. Hindus, Muslims of all sects, and a few Christians now reside in the 30 apartments there. No more Christmas star.

As for me, I moved to Dubai and have been here since 1997.

What happened in my teens before I came here, well, those are stories for another time.

Pakistan, Zindabad.

Acknowledgements

This book would not have been possible without the support, patience, and encouragement of several incredible people whose contributions have been invaluable not only to the writing of this memoir but to my life as a whole. Truly, it takes a village.

First and foremost, the greatest of thanks belong to my parents, the Late John Permal and Josephine Permal, whose love and guidance, occasional slaps and well-aimed slippers have shaped who I am. Thank you for your unwavering support and for the countless sacrifices you have made for me. Every word in this book is a testament to your belief in me. I love you.

To my siblings, Sue-Ellen and Adrian, thank you for the companionship, the bickering, the encouragement and the endless laughter I hope we'll share forever. Christopher, thank you for being a part of our family through Sue and for your continuous encouragement throughout my time writing this journey.

I am immensely grateful to my editors. Hamna Zubair, you helped right my ship and put me on a journey of growth and writing development, without which I wouldn't have learned what I know today; and Mehr Husain, your keen insight and attention to detail enhanced this work, and your patience and dedication have not gone unnoticed.

The guidance from both of you was the beacon that led me through the challenging process of storytelling and self-reflection.

My friends and loves, who throughout this journey gave me the feedback, critique and forgotten insights, and sometimes just the company I needed, you will never realise how much I appreciate all of you.

A special thank you to Fatima Bhutto, who was the first to see the initial words I penned and gave me the critique I needed at the time. Fatima helped me learn the difference between writing anything else and writing a book. Your advice forms the bedrock this memoir is built on.

Above all, I thank God for the countless blessings and for the strength, peace and self-belief bestowed upon me during the challenging moments of writing this memoir.

Each of you has left a mark on this work, and for that, I am eternally grateful.

About the author

Anthony J Permal is a Pakistani Catholic living in the United Arab Emirates.

Born in 1979 in Karachi, Pakistan, he spent his childhood years growing up in different towns in Karachi, as well as in the Saudi city of Dhahran. After attending university, he moved to Dubai in the UAE to be with his father, John, who wanted him to start a career in a country with better prospects for a young Christian boy. He became an Associate of the Chartered Institute of Marketing in 2014, and went on to carve a life in digital marketing. Today he is self-employed as a consultant to the pharmaceutical industry.

When he's not busy helping clients or copywriting for anyone who needs a hand at the written word, he enjoys curating his ever-growing collection of pop-culture items, including comics, merchandise, figures and collectors' editions or is busy traveling to discover more of the world. Anthony is currently working on his next book.

Printed in the USA
CPSIA information can be obtained
at www.ICGtesting.com
LVHW091037280824
789519LV00013B/137